"DADDY"
Andrew Charles "A.C." Williams Jr.
and his Teen Town Singers

"DADDY"

Andrew Charles "A.C." Williams Jr. and his Teen Town Singers

By
Wiley Henry

GrantHouse Publishers
2024

DEDICATION

To The Teen Town Singers who grew up and conquered
the world as singers, songwriters, entertainers,
entrepreneurs, educators, administrators, athletes,
and more, and never forgot their progenitor
— Andrew Charles "Moohah" Williams Jr. —
whom they affectionately called "Daddy."

Andrew Charles "A.C." Williams Jr.
December 7, 1916 – December 3, 2004

CONTENTS

FOREWORD

I grew up in Memphis listening to radio station WDIA without options. We were not allowed to touch the radio dial in our home. My mother, Corine Olivia Gray, enjoyed Ms. Willa Monroe, the gospel music and the sermons featuring various ministers.

My dad, the Reverend Leo M. Gray Sr., enjoyed the gospel music and sermons but made no apology for listening to Rufus Thomas, B.B. King, and Arnold Dwight "Gatemouth" Moore. They had an unwritten philosophy: "If WDIA doesn't play it, you don't need to hear it."

I learned to recognize the different air personalities by their voices. For example, Robert "Honey Boy" Thomas had a smooth flowing voice in which every word was distinct. Marth Jean "The Queen" Steinberg had a captivating voice that psychologically held her male listeners mesmerized and waiting to be seduced.

When Rufus "The Dog" Thomas came on the air, the listeners buckled their seat belts and waited for the punch lines. Ford Nelson had a velvet-like voice that informed the listeners with the latest news and public service announcements. Theo "Bless My Bones" Wade had the most unique voice in all of radio. His voice was arresting and convincing. Whatever the product or event he was promoting, the listeners were convinced it was the real deal.

Nat D. Williams had the reverberating voice of a Beale Street banker, selling products from the doorway of a store. His voice was authoritative and pregnant with racial pride and hope. Once you heard this voice and laugh, you never forgot to whom the voice belonged.

Then there was the voice of Andrew Charles Williams Jr., better known as A.C. "Moohah" Williams. As a young listener, whenever I heard his gutsy, rich voice, I would pay attention. His voice, undergirded with fatherly counsel, could not be ignored. I later learned the source of his impact. He had spent decades building credibility and trust in the Memphis community.

Mr. Williams was home-grown, having received his elementary and secondary education in the Memphis City Schools. After graduating from Booker T. Washington High School, he enrolled at Tennessee A&I State University, where he earned a bachelor's degree in agriculture.

Driven by a burning desire to give back to his community, he launched a stellar career in education. He taught agriculture in Whiteville, Tennessee, served as a school principal in Trenton, Tennessee, and taught biology at Manassas High School for eight years. His charismatic personality and generous spirit ingratiated him to hundreds of students and colleagues.

Following a celebrated tenure in education, the new owners of WDIA came calling for Mr. Williams to join them in the broadcasting industry. They were Bert Ferguson and John Pepper. They'd established a new radio station in Memphis in 1947, and the station was programmed initially for listeners of country and western music.

In marketing strategies, Ferguson and Pepper realized that a void was basically ignored over the airwaves and throughout the African American community. With no competition in Memphis, WDIA changed the program focus and became the first radio station in America programmed exclusively for the African American community.

The African American population in 1947 was too large to be ignored by the power structure of Memphis. In 1949, WDIA made a conscience decision to embrace the rich culture of African Americans in education, the blues, Memphis barbecue, the African American church, and Beale Street. Mr. Williams was the foundation of this strategy. He was the first full-time African American hired by WDIA. He made sure he was not the last.

For the next twenty years, WDIA's on-air personalities were overwhelmingly recruited from the ranks of Booker T. Washington High School alumni – Nat D. Williams, Robert "Honey Boy" Thomas, Dwight Arnold "Gatemouth" Moore, Rufus Thomas, Markhum Stansbury Sr., and Maurice Hubbard – and proudly displayed the green and gold of BTW Warriors.

Mr. Williams adopted the nickname "Moohah," which

means "mighty." He became a mighty force at WDIA and improved the welfare of African Americans. As the public relation director, he was solely responsible for staple programs benefiting the African American community.

His name was synonymous with the Starlite Revue and the Goodwill Revue, and major concerts featuring the likes of James Brown, B.B. King, Bobby "Blue" Bland, Sam Cooke, Ruth Brown, Aretha Franklin, and the Soul Stirrers. He promoted the Cotton Makers Jubilee, the United Negro College Fund, the Beale Street Elks Christmas Basket Annual Drive, WDIA Little League Baseball, and scholarships for Memphis youth.

In addition to his public relations duties, Mr. Williams hosted three unforgettable shows: "Saturday Night Fish Fry," "Wheeling on Beale," and "The Delta Melodies." He also produced a weekly show featuring local high school students, who were known as The Teen Town Singers.

From this group emerged Carla Thomas, Judge James Swearingen, Jesse Neely, Fred Davis, Robert "Honeymoon" Gardner, Markhum Stansbury Sr., James Nelson, and Ed Townsend. Cathryn Rivers Johnson served as the musical directress for this group and other adventures that required music.

Although Mr. Williams could not read nor write music, he wrote songs for local artists and collaborated with rising stars at STAX and SUN recording studios. He would hum the melody until Robert "Honeymoon" Gardner or Cathryn Rivers Johnson would write down the musical notes. His most famous collaboration was with Roy Orbison on his song "Pretty Woman."

Mr. Williams was honored numerous times but not nearly enough. He received numerous awards and citations from civic, political, and religious organizations. He served on the Board of the National Civil Rights Museum, and chaired local campaigns for the United Negro College Fund, Inc.

He also provided noble leadership to the board of the Goodwill Fund and organized the Community Advisory Board for WDIA in the late seventies. (On a personal note, I was selected to serve on the board and study Mr. Williams from close-up.)

What the community felt, needed, and wanted mattered greatly to A.C. Williams. His service to the community was so extensive the Salem Gilfield Baptist Church, led by the Reverend Charles Ryan, established the A.C. Williams Community Service Award in 2004.

Mr. Williams was committed to his family, God, and his church. He was an active member of Salem Gilfield for 76 years, where he served as chairman of the deacon board, a trustee, choir director, and a master Sunday school teacher.

Throughout his professional journey, Mr. Williams enjoyed the ever-present support of his devoted wife, Atee Williams; his daughter Joan Williams Patterson; a son, Andrew (Sonny) James; a stepson, Willie Lee Wiley; and a stepdaughter, Dorothy Alexander. Family truly mattered to Mr. Williams.

On Friday, December 3, 2004, A.C. "Moohah" Williams finished his earthly assignment to hear his Heavenly Father

declare unto him: "Well done thy good and faithful servant."
Mr. Williams, in signing off, did not drop his mike; he passed
it on to the next generation.

WDIA is known as the heartbeat of the Memphis
community. We now know that A.C. "Moohah" Williams was
the heartbeat of WDIA.

Dr. L. LaSimba M. Gray Jr.
November 2023

FOREWORD

Growing up listening to radio there was always certain personalities that would stand out or you would always remember what they had to say on the radio. One such personality was A.C. "Moohah" Williams of WDIA. Usually, when you heard an on-air personality and especially if it was a man, you could hear a deep sexy tone that would make you cringe in your seat or leave you so mesmerized you never wanted to turn them or the station off. But when it came to A.C. "Moohah" Williams, you heard an education man, a man with strong convictions, a man of faith, and a voice for the community and of the community.

My remembrance of Mr. Williams, listening to him on WDIA, was first hearing him come on with the WDIA Teen Town Singers and instructing them, and wishing that I was a part of that group since I loved to sing. My second remembrance of Mr. Williams was listening to him do commercials, and how convincing he was that you would go out and buy that product immediately. One such product that comes to mind are the Tide commercials. After Mr. Williams would describe the product and what it had to offer, he would end by saying, "Go out and buy Tide Ta-Day," mispronouncing the word Today. I always got a kick out of that one line because you knew he meant business.

I had the pleasure and privilege of working with Mr. Williams when I was hired at WDIA in 1983; he was then doing the morning gospel show. He was always very polite, cordial, and complimentary of me and the work that I was doing. He reminded me that WDIA was a Goodwill station and to make sure that I work in and for the community. I was very happy to know that he respected me. When you read this book about A.C. "Moohah" Williams, I hope you get an insight of a man who had the community at heart as well as a station he truly loved dearly — WDIA.

Bev Johnson
Talk Show Host
WDIA Radio

PREFACE

The song was ethereal, permeating, and indeed a fitting selection for a beloved man who was remembered by an entire community for his contributions in education, radio and community service. So, when the choir at Salem Gilfield Baptist Church in Memphis, Tennessee — where Andrew Charles "A.C." Williams Jr. had been a longtime member — sang "Order My Steps in Your Word," one could almost envision the steps that God had ordered for Mr. Williams throughout his lifetime.

> Order my steps in Your word, dear Lord
> Lead me, guide me everyday
> Send Your anointing, Father I pray
> Order my steps in Your word
> Please, order my steps in Your word

The day of Mr. Williams's homegoing — Saturday, December 11, 2004 — was replete with wonderful remembrances and heartfelt expressions from those who knew him intimately and loved him dearly. It was a celebration worthy of a man who walked tall and whose eminence was like sunshine that warmed the hearts of the bereaved. The rays penetrated the entire sanctuary and radiated throughout the community among the people that Mr. Williams loved dearly — particularly young people.

He taught agriculture at the Allen-White High School in Whiteville, Tennessee, biology at Manassas High School for eight years, and served as principal at Rosenwald High School in Trenton, Tennessee. In radio, he was triumphant as the first fulltime African-American disc jockey and public relations director for WDIA 1070 AM Radio Station.

In both careers, Mr. Williams impacted the lives of thousands of listeners over the airwaves and enriched the lives of many school-aged children that he taught in school.

He founded a choral group in 1949 called The Teen Town Singers that he corralled from inner city high schools in Memphis and Shelby County. He enriched their lives as well.

WDIA's listening audience knew Mr. Williams by his adopted call name, "Moohah," an Indian name meaning "mighty," when he served for more than three decades as an influential radio personality who lit up the airwaves. He was a jovial, fun-loving jock who promoted, for example, the Starlite Revue and the Goodwill Revue, the radio station's signature events.

Mr. Williams was the Black community's go-to person and the lynchpin that connected the radio station to a growing Black listening audience. He also used the platform to introduce The Teen Town Singers to the Mid-South and the world, for that matter, and provided them with opportunities to perform on radio and throughout the community.

He was loved by the young, impressionable Teen Town Singers who referred to him as "Daddy," a term of endearment that held them together in an affectionate bond.

He was, in a sense, an honorary member of their families.

He was dapper, a towering figure, tough, God-fearing; and most of all, he was a man of principle who accepted his role as "Daddy," their surrogate father, their protector, their progenitor. Some of the teens no doubt longed for their own fathers, perhaps, due to some extenuating circumstances. But Mr. Williams didn't mind filling the void that was left vacant by a few absentee fathers.

Memories abound, and Mr. Williams's legacy has endured for decades, from generation to generation. Throughout his life and professional career, "Moohah" was the "mighty" one indeed, a man whose steps were ordered by the omnipotent God, whom Mr. Williams had served faithfully. In addition to being a man of principle, he was a man of faith, integrity, and trusted God with his life, his career, and with the young people in his charge.

The Teen Town Singers and the hundreds of young people he taught in area schools, and the countless youth he mentored, were receptive to his love, nurturing, devotion, and his commitment to them. Why? He developed them, promoted them as individuals, and loved them collectively.

He left an indelible mark on their lives in general and on his beloved community collectively. The Teen Town Singers — those who are still with us — continue to carry within their hearts a deep and abiding love and precious memories for the man they affectionately called "Daddy," a man who helped to build their self-esteem, lift their spirits, and prepare them for the world at large.

He was the incomparable Mr. Williams, whom The Teen Town Singers still hold in high esteem decades after his death. They have not forgotten the man they called "Daddy."

New Park Cemetery in Memphis is Mr. Williams's final resting place. He left behind his wife, Mrs. Attee Williams; a daughter, Joan E. Patterson; a son, Willie Wiley of Ontario, California; 12 grandchildren; 22 great grandchildren; and a bevy of Teen Town Singers.

Memories of Mr. Williams are etched in their hearts.

1

Family Matters

Sometimes life stories are better told by those who live it, or when it's written by their own hand and left behind for posterity. The story then comes to life, and one would clearly see the motivation that moves him or her to succeed in life, one's parentage, and the place from whence the writer hails.

Such was the case with Andrew Charles "A.C." Williams Jr., who provided written answers to questions about his life, his parents, and his maternal and paternal grandparents, which were posed by someone he identified as "Sue Z." The year was 1990. In his own words — some of them he underlined for emphasis — he began with the salutation.

Dear Sue Z (I like that):

It was so wonderful to spin a <u>few hours</u> with you and Eric (even on a sad occasion). I was happy to see both of you and to know you're doing Ok. I have seen Joan and Chuck several times since I've seen both of you. I hope Tee and I can remedy that when you get moved and settled.

Wiley Henry

Now to answer your questions.

1) My paternal grandmother was <u>Jennie Williams</u>. Native home Somerville, Tennessee, but lived most of her life in Memphis. She had <u>smooth black skin</u> and <u>white hair</u> (white as snow). She was <u>beautiful</u>!! Paternal grand- father – <u>I never knew him</u>. My maternal grandmother was Margaret Saunders. My maternal grandfather was James Saunders. (They both lived and died around Courtland, Alabama).

2) My <u>father</u> was born in Somerville, Tennessee, Came to Memphis when he was 11 years old and was self-supported from then until he died. Worked as a houseboy in a jewelry store and for <u>The Union Station Co.</u> until he died. He was always neat, clean, well-dressed. Wore a suit and tie to work (on the trolley) every day. Changed to <u>coveralls</u> to work in. When he got off work, he took a shower, put his suit and tie back on and came home. His name was Andrew Williams, Sr. (I am a Jr.).

3) My mother's maiden name was <u>Angie Saunders</u>. Born in Courtland, Alabama. Came to Memphis and went to work as a domestic. Met my father, married, had <u>one child</u> (me), and did not spoil me (smile)! She was a beautiful woman (both inside and out). She was a <u>devout Christian</u> who taught me to fear God and <u>carried</u> me to S.S. (Sunday School) and church. My mother had less than a third-grade education, but she <u>solved the problems</u> brought to her from all the neighbors.

She helped those in need around her. She never failed to share with her neighbors, and by her example, she taught me that we are all God's children, therefore, sisters and brothers bound together by an unbreakable cord, which is <u>God's love</u>. She <u>lived</u> it every day!!

(Sue, if this paper is wet, it's because you've got me crying, reminiscing about my mother and father in a way I have not done in years. We were like three children in a house together. And my mother was the closet I['ve] ever gotten to an <u>Angel</u>).

4) My father was an only child (as I was). My mother had <u>one sister</u> and <u>one brother</u>. (The brother lived to get 100 years old).

5) Neither of my parents were educated. But they had a home bought and paid for by the time I was 4 years old, and I lived in that home until I graduated from college.

Tee says welcome to the pictures and sends her love to you, Eric and our "<u>greats</u>." Kiss Eric for us and hug <u>Vonique</u> and <u>Chris</u> real tight. Also say hello to your mother and tell her to keep in touch. (I read all of her letters to Tee).

I love You!!

Granddaddy

P.S. Eric: I don't have to tell you that I love you. You have known that all your life! We pray for all four of you night and day.

2

A Popular Entrée For WDIA

A C.Williams Jr. and his Teen Town Singers, a choral group that he started in 1949, were off to a good start with the backing of WDIA-AM 1070, the first radio station in the country to feature all-Black programing and on-air personalities.

Their voices, melding together harmoniously, were now reverberating across the airwaves into the homes of countless listeners who approved of the station's newest program offering.

The teen program proved to be a popular entrée for WDIA and a boon for Williams. It also benefited the aspiring teens who needed the station's platform to sharpen and test the power of their soaring and melodious vocals before a radio listening audience.

The road to WDIA began at Manassas High School, where Williams was teaching biology and where he first started working with the choral group. He spent eight years in the classrooms at Manassas before the doors to WDIA opened to his Teen Town Singers.

In the early days, WDIA was located at 2074 Union

Avenue, where the blues, gospel and R&B were attracting a burgeoning Black listening audience, even though the Black population in Memphis in the late 1940s and early '50s was around 40 percent.

To show his appreciation, Charles Smith, an original member of the teen choral group, penned a personal thank you note to Williams. It read in part:

"Again, I wish to thank you for all that you've done for me. I wish you would drop me a line sometimes. Having no more to write, I guess I'll say so long 'til later."

Your young protégé
Charles Smith

The rollout of WDIA's new teen program was generating a considerable amount of attention in Memphis and the Mid-South and catching the eyes of the roving media. Newspaper headlines introducing The Teen Town Singers to a wider audience were printed in bold fonts to catch the eyes of the curious reader.

In *The Memphis World*, for example, a screaming headline drew readers directly into the story, which was printed in the newspaper's June 1949 edition: "Teen Town Singers New Program On Station WDIA."

The Memphis World, an African-American newspaper, was founded in 1931. Its editor was the noted journalist Lewis Ossie Swingler, or L.O. Swingler, who also served a stint as editor-in-chief and co-publisher of the weekly *Tri-State Defender*, an African-American newspaper still in operation today in Memphis.

In a sense, the first two paragraphs of the story in *The Memphis World* newspaper unveiled to readers an emergent choral group on the rise with a promising future.

> A new program, called Teen Singers, featuring the talent from High Schools in the city, started last Saturday at 4 p.m. over Radio Station WDIA.
>
> To be heard every Saturday at this time, the program will be directed by Mr. Andrew C. Williams, instructor at Manassas High School, who will also serve as master of ceremonies.

The story went on to say that children in the Mid-South "have been invited to attend" weekly auditions on Tuesday and Thursday mornings at 10 a.m. at Manassas High School. Auditions began in June before and after the official launch of the teen program.

In another newspaper story, published Tuesday, August 30, 1949, a young Teen Towner was awarded a scholarship. His voice, ringing out over the airwaves of WDIA, was the deciding factor.

> A 15-year-old negro boy [George Koen, a freshman at Hamilton High School] has won a high school and college scholarship with Rust College, Holly Springs, Miss., after being heard singing on a tenn-age [sic] program over WDIA.

The popularity that The Teen Town Singers had enjoyed since its founding was now sizzling over the airwaves. But then the program went off the air during the summer of 1950; it resumed in the fall, however. A sponsor was needed to ensure the program's survival. One such sponsor, secured in March 1951, was the Universal Life Insurance Company.

The Memphis-based company was established September 6, 1923, by Dr. J.E. Walker, the former president of Mississippi Life Insurance Company. In 1947, Universal Life Insurance Company was considered one of the Top Ten "Negro" business enterprises in the world. In 1952, A. Maceo Walker succeeded his father as president.

The company was actively involved in the African-American community and took its civic responsibility serious. Its reach in the community was widespread and its presence was greatly felt.

The company's assets were used for civic improvements, mortgage funds, and community engagement, such as providing scholarships to deserving youngsters.

Williams, for the most part, had secured one of the teen program's most ardent supporters. The relationship that was forged between WDIA and Universal Life Insurance Company would become integral to the teen program's success and longevity over a span of years.

Aside from Williams's pet project — his beloved Teen Town Singers — and WDIA providing the platform for the teens to showcase their vocal chops and melodic sound, the success of the teen program could be measured by the number of scholarships that were doled out to the teens attending college or a university.

George Koen, of course, was able to attend Rust College

after a college official heard him singing over the airwaves. He was awarded a seven-year scholarship (three years to finish high school and four years to attend Rust College). So, he benefited immensely as a member of Williams's choral group.

Other Teen Towners receiving scholarships and awards were Jesse Neely, who earned a one-year scholarship in music to Kentucky State College, and James Earl Swearengen, who was tapped for a one-year scholarship to Kentucky State College as well.

Irby Cox, for example, spent two years with the Tuskegee Institute Choir and was elected its president for 1952 and 1953. During this time, he'd completed two visits to New York and made an appearance on television. He credited Williams and The Teen Town Singers program with helping him to become a choir member.

Another Teen Towner, Earl Townsend, would go on to teach school. He also took a part-time job as a disc jockey in Hot Springs, Arkansas, where he organized a group of youngsters and likewise named them Teen Town Singers.

Good fortunate had smiled on other Teen Towners as well because of their participation in the choral group and their affiliation with Williams. In fact, it was Williams's influence and contacts with Tennessee State University that made it possible for Webster Williamson, Joseph Williams, Charles Smith, and Norma Jean Ford to receive "work aid."

With Williams at the helm directing The Teen Town

Singers and with Cathryn Rivers Johnson assisting him and accompanying the group as their pianist, the Teen Towners would continue to make headway in music and entertainment. It was a whole new world of infinite possibilities for Williams and his choral group.

For the most part, Williams and Johnson — who taught at Booker T. Washington High School and was the musician for Salem Gilfield Baptist Church where Williams worshiped — were a formidable twosome that the surviving Teen Towners continue to esteem and credit decades later for enriching their lives.

"She had that kind of respect from the children that they would do something when Mrs. Johnson said do it. That was her strength, in terms of her work," Patricia Howard, then executive director of Girls Inc., said about Johnson in a news story about her death in the February 4, 1995, issue of *The Commercial Appeal* newspaper.

"She had a way of talking to them, and they understood what she meant. She would do anything she could for them," Howard continued.

Markhum "Mark" L. Stansbury Sr., then the interim president of the former Shelby State Community College and a former Teen Town Singer himself, noted that Johnson was an inspiration to him while he was a student at Booker T. Washington High School and after he'd graduated. She often wrote to him and sent a few dollars for encouragement as well, he pointed out in the news story.

Elsie Bailey remembered Johnson always being "involved with the students. I guess that's why she stayed so youthful," said Bailey, a former BTW principal and student of Johnson in her 10th grade class in 1957. She also sang with The Teen Town Singers.

Irma Jeffrey, a BTW guidance counselor, recalled Johnson helping "disadvantaged students prepare for college" and helping "students get scholarships to attend summer math and science programs at college campuses around the country."

After teaching music and English at BTW for more than twenty years, Johnson retired and took a job as an educational talent search counselor for Girl's Inc., Teen Challenge program. Howard said Johnson, who had come to work at Girl's Inc. about seven years before her death, missed being involved with students. They were her life, she said.

Johnson was a board member of the National Civil Rights Museum, the WDIA Goodwill Fund, and Project RAP. She also was a lifetime member of Alpha Kappa Alpha and the NAACP. She left an enduring legacy at 68 years old and an indelible mark on so many children under her tutelage.

3

Engineering A Clean Sweep

One might say that A.C. Williams Jr. was positioned to make a lateral move from teaching biology at Manassas High School to joining the staff at WDIA in 1949 as the radio station's point man for community affairs and public relations.

The lateral move was in fact a gargantuan leap for Williams, who began utilizing his skills set to help catapult WDIA into a megawatt radio station—50,000 watts to be exact — which would inevitably seal his fate in the annals of broadcasting history.

While Williams was making headway at WDIA, the first radio station in the United States that was programed entirely for African Americans, his reputation was growing exponentially as well. He was now WDIA's first full-time Black employee and, overseeing various programs, endeared himself to the African-American community.

But before Williams joined the staff at WDIA, the radio station had switched from country and western music to all-Black on-air personalities and programming to expand its listening audience in Memphis, i.e., the Bluff City, where the meandering Mississippi River ebbs and flows along the embankment of cobblestones on the fringes of downtown Memphis.

Owned by John R. Pepper and Bert Ferguson, WDIA was having difficulty establishing its footprint in the Memphis market and competing with five other radio stations in the city after sputtering as a "hillbilly station." Ratings had plummeted. The owners had to do something radically different to keep from closing the doors and staving off foreclosing.

It was a historic move on the part of Pepper and Ferguson, whose former listeners of country and western music did not understand or appreciate WDIA's reasons for engineering a clean sweep in programming and all-Black on-air personalities.

It was a foregone conclusion that Whites detested the radical move and a fact that their detestation, it was reported, had materialized into threats of violence. At that time, violence wouldn't have been too far-fetched, considering that Memphis was in the throes of the civil rights movement and racial tension was seething.

No one could have known what Pepper and Ferguson had been thinking. However, it's safe to assume that it was a business decision to overhaul the station, to increase its slumping ratings, and to shore up the station's miserable bottom line. It was, after all, a matter of survival — WDIA's life or death. Pepper and Ferguson chose life.

Though A.C. Williams Jr. was WDIA's first Black fulltime hire, it was Nat. D. Williams, a beloved history teacher at Booker T. Washington High School, who broke the color barrier at WDIA and made it possible for other Black radio personalities to follow his lead.

The owners first hired the affable Nat D. to emcee a one-hour show on October 25, 1948, from 4-5 p.m. It was called "Tan Town Jamboree." The show was a success. More than 5,000 letters poured into the station within a couple of days after the show had aired.

For Nat D., success was imminent. He was in his element at the microphone when the owners tapped him for that explicit purpose alone. A natural showman, it was his broadcasting of "Amateur Nite on Beale Street" from the old Palace Theatre that aroused Pepper and Ferguson and convinced them to take a chance on Nat D.

WDIA's lease on life was now renewed. In 1949, the station rose to No. 2 in the Memphis market. Nat D., as he was affectionately known by hundreds of thousands of listeners, had proven that a Black man could turn the tide of the once failing white-owned radio station.

Not only was Nat D. making waves at WDIA, he was also creating raves with his nationally syndicated column called "Down on Beale" for *The Pittsburgh Courier, The Memphis World, The Tri-State Defender,* and other Black publications. He wrote about current events through the eyes of different characters on Beale Street in a whimsical and folksy writing style.

Williams tipped his hat to Nat D. when he was asked to speak about the station's first Black disc jockey at a forum attended by officials from the Smithsonian Institution. He told them, plain and simple, that Nat D. was "one of the most unsung but deserving real heroes of Memphis and the Mid-South."

It was Nat D.'s wit, humor, gift of gab, infectious laugh, and his comedic approach to deejaying that was proven to be the right ingredients that had been missing prior to WDIA's transition to all-Black programing and on-air personalities.

So, one would suspect that the so-called Black experiment that Pepper and Ferguson first tested with Nat D. was, in effect, a shot in the arm that was needed to revive the near comatose radio station. It was the right decision, as it turned out.

Because of Nat D.'s success — whose work at the console was sending ratings upward and expanding WDIA's reach in the Black community — his one-hour show was increased to two hours. Then a morning show — the "Tan Town Coffee Club" — was added to the 6:30 a.m. - 8 a.m. time slot.

Within less than six months, all the station's on-air personalities were Black, even though the administration, helmed by Pepper and Ferguson, was all White, except for Williams, the first Black man to move into administration, the first to assume a leadership role at WDIA.

Following Nat D. to the broadcasting desk and audio console, with daily programs added to the mix, were Maurice "Hot Rod" Hulbert, the Reverend Dwight "Gatemouth" Moore, and Willa Monroe, the South's first Black female broadcaster who became the "Tan Town Homemaker."

While Nat D. was causing ripples of excitement at the console, with approval from WDIA's owners, of course, Williams was moving full speed ahead himself with his Teen Town Singers. The half-hour show on Saturdays was only the beginning of Williams's creative input at the station.

In the early 1950s, Williams developed a program that he described as "pure, unadulterated Country Blues." It was called "Wheeling On Beale." In words he'd written on paper, Williams explained the program's plot to the forum's attendees, including the officials from the Smithsonian, when he was touting Nat D.'s groundbreaking work at WDIA.

The story was fictional. Williams had a bit part in the program as "Mister Blues," the executive secretary for Lightning Hopkins, president of "The Royal Amalgamated Association of Chitterling Eaters of America for The Preservation of Good Country Blues," which licensed the program. Muddy Waters served as vice president.

A "mythical convention" was held each year in Town Creek, Alabama, at which time rules, regulations and alcohol consumption were discussed, Williams explained. A guitar, piano, and drums — used as instrumental backing on records — were only allowed to be played on this program. If a record had brass or reed instruments, it was outlawed.

Live artists appeared on the program with Williams, each one having a fifteen-minute slot. They were Joe Hill Louis, The Be Bop Boy, performing three times per week. Louis, Williams wrote, used both feet to keep rhythm on a bass drum and a clap cymbal.

Louis "had a harness that fitted around his neck and held a harmonica, which he blew in-between vocals, which he sang. All of this was going on at once," Williams wrote, noting that Louis "got a lot of 'gigs' in and around Memphis."

Dr. Ross and The Internes: Dr. Ross's four-piece blues band was based in Tunica, Mississippi, and drove up to Memphis to appear on WDIA each Wednesday at 1:15 p.m. Dr. Ross was the medical director for the Royal Amalgamated Association, Williams wrote. He left Memphis and moved to Terre Haute, Indiana, and in later years made a couple of European tours.

Barber Parker and The Silver Kings: Parker was the drummer in Dr. Ross's band, Williams noted, and when he left the South, Parker took over the band and continued the weekly appearances on WDIA for the next ten years. "When asked why his band was called The Silver Kings, he would reply, 'Everywhere they played, the proprietor would always lock up all the loose silverware.'"

Blues recording artists whose records met the qualifications for programing on "Wheeling On Beale" included — in addition to Lightning Hopkins and Muddy Waters — Sonny Boy Williamson, Howling Wolf, Little Jr. Parker, Jimmy Reed, and Little Son Jackson, whose "Rock Me Mana" (sic) inspired BB. King's big hit of the same tune.

Williams also had a program on WDIA titled "Saturday Night Fish Fry." The hours were from 4-7 p.m. on Saturdays and featured urban blues and the whole gamut of music included in the rhythm and blues library of the 1950s. The theme song was recorded by Louis Jordan and it, too, was called "Saturday Night Fish Fry."

The music of Chuck Willis, Amos Milburn, Charles Brown, and early Ray Charles records were standard fare on the show, including the big band sounds of Duke Ellington, Count Basie, Buddy Johnson, and others. Live bands included Al Jackson, Sr. and his 12-piece outfit. His son, Al Jackson, Jr., was the drummer for Booker T. and the M.G.'s and the Markeys during the glory days at Stax Records. A local blues band, headed by Red Saunders, was added to the program as well. Saunders wrote a song called "Crosscut Saw." Albert King made the song a big hit.

"Saturday Night Fish Fry" was a "real wild one," Williams noted. "'WDIA's Saturday Night Fish Fry' took its title from an event that used to happen every Saturday night in the neighborhood where I grew up, which was known as Willett Bottom. In Willett Bottom, they would have an outdoor fish fry every Saturday night...and if somebody didn't get killed...they'd have it over on

Sunday."

The blues was a staple at WDIA, a standard fare, even during the years when rock and roll competed for the attention of young listeners whose taste in music varied. Still, the station kept churning out the blues each Saturday morning for three solid hours, featuring the likes of B.B. King, Bobby Blue Bland, Albert King, and Z.Z. Hill.

It's also worth mentioning that Williams's "Saturday Night Fish Fry" could be described as a training ground for young jocks like Bill Terrell, Wash Allen, and Herb Kneeland. In addition to Willa Monroe, the other female broadcaster that reigned at WDIA was the "Queen" herself, Martha Jean Steinberg, who joined the staff of A-listed deejays in 1954. During her heyday, she'd become very influential and the crème de la crème in the Memphis community and beyond.

Williams hosted other programs for WDIA as well, including "Delta Melodies," and "Payday Today," a skit where he'd transform into "Moohah," the "Mighty One." His labor was not in vain — for success followed him each step of his journey at WDIA and throughout the community that he served faithfully and loved so well.

Here was a man on the move.

4

WDIA: The Goodwill Station

In addition to his hosting duties at WDIA and directing The Teen Town Singers — including rigorous weekly rehearsals — A.C. Williams Jr. took on the awesome responsibility of overseeing the promotions of WDIA's annual Goodwill Revue, which kicked off in 1949, the year he was brought onboard as the station's point-man for promotions.

The Starlite Revue was another community event garnering widespread attention that Williams also promoted under the auspices of WDIA. Presented by WDIA's Goodwill Fund, Incorporated, which was created in part by Williams, the Starlite Revue began in 1954 to aid poor and disadvantaged "Negro" children in need of a helping hand.

The Goodwill Revue and the Starlite Revue were both charitable events for the station. Entertainment was supplied by Williams, the public relations director, who culled talent for both events from a wellspring of some of the best local and national acts, including the slate of deejays from WDIA's roster.

One hundred percent of monies raised from both revues were used to help needy Black families, transport disabled

Black children to school, sponsor Little League Baseball, dole out money to help families put food on the table, and establish the Goodwill Home for Black Children. None of the money was used for operating expenses.

In fact, Black children were transported to and from events on white "WDIA Goodwill Buses" throughout Memphis — to Little League Baseball games, for example. Their sponsorship of the "games" began and continued after the Memphis Park Commission had initially asked the station to step up to the plate and sponsor one Little League Baseball team. WDIA happily offered to sponsor all the teams, which numbered more than 100 teams.

Always in a mode of community service and willing to support the marginalized Black community in Memphis and the Mid-South, the station raised $40,000 — seed money if you will — to get Goodwill Boys Club of Memphis started and another $10,000 to purchase equipment. WDIA didn't stop there. In fact, the "Goodwill Station," as it was christened in the early days, continued to contribute to worthy causes benefiting the Black community.

Another $40,000 was earmarked for Dixie Homes Goodwill Boys' Club. — which was a pledge from WDIA to support the boys club. But after a question was raised about doing something to benefit girls, the station didn't hesitate to dole out another $40,000 to undergird St. Thomas Girls' Club.

Since the launch of WDIA in 1947 — which began as a White station offering classical, light pop, and country and western music —an infusion of capital and a total revamping of the operation would soon be needed to save

WDIA from going belly-up.

In retrospect, the Black community would become the recipient of WDIA's renewed focus on community service and activities for the least of the station's listening audience. The Black community had become in fact the station's targeted audience, which benefited immensely from its "goodwill" activities.

Over time, WDIA's airwaves had begun reverberating with programs that sparked acute interest from a groundswell of Black listeners. Much of what was happening for WDIA — in terms of the station's cozy relationship with the Black community — was due in part to its continued effort to build upon its foundation of community service.

Community service had essentially become the cornerstone of WDIA's success in the marketplace and the "strong and authoritative Black voice in the Mid-South," which catapulted the station to a higher plateau that other radio stations around the country sought to emulate.

The rise of WDIA had not gone unnoticed. The station was making a difference in the Black community and served a clientele that reciprocated by keeping the dial on their radio locked into WDIA's frequency. Other stations were tuning in perhaps to gain a competitive edge. They wanted to know what WDIA was doing to turn the tide of a once-declining radio station before its transformation.

In 1954, WDIA increased its power from 250 to 50,000 watts and moved from 730 kHz to a frequency of 1070 kHz. The signal was now powerful enough to reach the Mississippi Delta, the Missouri Bootheel, and the Gulf

Coast. According to Louis Cantor's "Wheelin' on Beale: How WDIA Memphis Became the Nation's First All-Black Radio Station and Created the Sound That Changed America," WDIA had reached 10 percent of the African-American population in the United States.

WDIA had secured its place in history. Its popularity was undeniable and the impact in the Black community was huge. The station, it seemed, was on a trajectory that was unstoppable. But then the fate of WDIA was left hanging in the balance after Egmont Sonderling of Sonderling Broadcasting Corporation purchased the station in 1957.

Sonderling had immigrated to the United States from Germany in 1923. At its peak, Sonderling Broadcasting Corporation had owned eleven radio stations in major markets across the country, a television company, and an independent chain of theaters comprising a total of 55 screens. A resident of Bal Harbour, Florida, Sonderling died in 1997 at the age of 91.

WDIA continued to thrive, thanks in part to the contributions of A.C. Williams and other pioneers who helped to usher in a new era in radio for the Black listening audience. Ford Nelson, who joined WDIA in 1950, told a reporter at *The Tri-State Defender* in a 2004 news story that the Black listening audience rallied around the luminaries of WDIA. Williams, of course, was one of them. The others were Nat D. Williams, a biology teacher at Booker T. Washington High School; Dwight "Gatemouth" Moore, an ordained minister, community leader, and songwriter who sang blues and gospel; and Maurice "Hot Rod" Hulbert, Jr., who came to WDIA in 1949.

They were the station's four major players — the frontrunners — and the first to break the color barrier, Nelson pointed out. He'd given [A.C.] Williams a nod as the "disc jockey" who had influenced him the most at WDIA, whom John R. Pepper and Bert Ferguson had hired as the standard bearer for public relations.

"Before us, you didn't hear much Black music on radio. Oh, maybe a local station would play Cab Calloway or Duke Ellington once every 4 hours or so. But that was it," said Williams, reflecting on his career in radio in the October 22, 1978, Sunday edition of *The Commercial Appeal Mid-South Magazine.*

WDIA had made significant contributions in the Memphis and Mid-South community and throughout the Mississippi Delta, the Missouri Bootheel, and the Gulf Coast, where 50,000 watts of power extended the station's reach and influence within the Black community and elsewhere across the country.

In 1969, for example, WDIA won Billboard's "Station of the Year Award." A year later, the National Association of Television and Radio Announcers also bestowed upon WDIA the "Radio Station of the Year" award. The honors and awards — citing WDIA for its importance in history and seemingly its impenetrable niche in the media — were continually heaped upon a radio station whose programs and community activities had never wavered.

In 1972, Charles Scruggs took over the reins of leadership at WDIA as its general manager and vice president. He was the first African American to hold such a lofty position at the radio station since its founding by

John R. Pepper and Bert Ferguson 25 years earlier.

During that time, Scruggs — also known as the affable "Mr. Chuck" on WKNO Public Television for nearly two decades — played a major role in raising money to save the Lorraine Motel, including securing a personal loan. His handy work behind the microphone, community engagement, and fundraising prowess helped to transform the motel in 1991 into the National Civil Rights Museum, which he co-founded.

Scruggs's tenure at WDIA lasted 12 years. However, the station would undergo additional changes in ownership — to Viacom International (1980 to 1983) and then to Clear Channel Communications (1996), which was rebranded as iHeart Media, WDIA's current owner.

Scruggs died in 2013 at the age of 80.

WDIA AM 1070 has much to celebrate. Its longevity, in addition to its success, couldn't have been possible without its early pioneers, such as Nat. D. Williams, Maurice "Hot Rod" Hulbert, the Reverend Dwight "Gatemouth" Moore, Willa Monroe, Ford Nelson, B.B. King, Rufus Thomas, Martha Jean "The Queen" Steinberg, Markhum Stansbury, A.C. "Moohah" Williams, and others.

The legacy lives on through WDIA's current on-air personalities: Bev Johnson, Stormy Taylor, Mike Evans, Tracy Bethea, Stan Bell "The Bellringer," and others. The legendary Bobby O'Jay, WDIA's longtime program director, was a radio pioneer himself. He died in 2022.

Known by its tagline — "The Heart & Soul of Memphis" — WDIA is still referred to as "The Goodwill Station."

5

The Church Was A.C. Williams's Anchor

What A.C. Williams Jr. was able to accomplish as an educator, community servant, and as a highly respected and beloved radio personality was due in large part to his work in the church and his unyielding and abiding faith in God, whom he served untiringly throughout his life with reverence and exceeding joy.

Williams was a longtime member of the historic Salem Gilfield Baptist Church, which began in late 1865 as the original Salem Church. Founded by the Reverend Africa Bailey, a sergeant in the Union Army during the raging Civil War, the members worshiped and praised God on a sawdust floor in a Brush Arbor.

By 1867, the church had increased its membership to over 200 members and began worshiping in a solid frame building at the corner of Carolina Street and Tennessee. In 1940, Salem merged with the old Gilfield Baptist Church and became Salem Gilfield Baptist Church.

The church has had a succession of pastors since its founding by the Reverend Africa Bailey. Following him to the pulpit were the reverends Dr. Jay, J. W. Ribbons, R. E. Harshaw, C. H. Hayes, Heard, J. M. Booker, Echols,

Williams Winston, R. B. Roberts, W. L. Varnado, A. L. McCargo, L. A. Wakefield, Charles H. Ryans Sr., Angelo McBride, and finally Stanford L. Hunt.

The Spirit dwells in the church and permeates the hearts of its believers, clergymen would often espouse from the pulpit — even during the early days when Williams, then in his youth, became a member. He was a believer indeed and looked to the Spirit to guide him throughout his career as an educator and at WDIA, where he rose to prominence and throughout his Christian journey as a servant of God.

In fact, Williams served faithfully until his death. He worshiped at only one church — Salem Gilfield Baptist Church, where he and his family occupied more than just the pews. In fact, the Williamses were willing workers and engaged in various church activities.

"Dad was born in that church," said Joan E. Patterson, Williams's daughter. She was raised in the church — she had to be there — because her father and mother insisted. Her mother, Joan H. Williams, played piano for Salem Gilfield and sang too. She was an operatic singer, Patterson noted, whose voice was golden and reverberated from one venue to another.

She said her mother's octaves were impressive and believed she was good enough to sing professionally. She even compared her voice to the legendary Marian Anderson's, who sang contralto and performed a wide range of music from opera to spirituals.

"She [Joan Herrisse Romby Williams] was a concert soloist and sang around the city [of Memphis]. She was a contralto and tried out for the Metropolitan; she loved classical music," Patterson imparted. "They used to come down periodically to look for talent; they came down for her. She almost took it, but she didn't want to leave us."

Church is where it all began for Patterson, who sang there and elsewhere — starting at Salem Gilfield under her mother's tutelage. And Williams's too — for his commitment to Salem Gilfield was just as taxing and as arduous as his duties at WDIA, and just as challenging in his role as founder and director of The Teen Town Singers.

At Salem Gilfield, Williams served as a deacon, trustee, Sunday School teacher, Division Superintendent, and chairman of the Mid-Week Prayer and Praise Service. In addition to his work in the church, Williams was known to organize programs using WDIA talent.

"I remember him putting on a mock radio program at the church and deejays came over," said Patterson. "They had parts like they were working at the radio station. He invited celebrities, and money that was raised went to the church."

Plays were performed at the church as well, said Patterson, an avid participant. "The church was where I learned 'The Messiah,'" she said, and explained that "The Messiah" is an oratorio that was compiled from the King James Bible and composed by George Frideric Handel in 1741.

"The Messiah is a book of Psalms from the scriptures," she added. "Handel wrote it in such a short time. The whole book of scriptures was put to song. I learned that at Salem Gilfield because our choir director was serious about classical music."

Williams was just as serious and broad-minded about

all genres of music. But more importantly, he was a man after God's own heart, and service was his reward. And Salem Gilfield Baptist Church? He and the church — his anchor — were inextricably linked.

6

Deriving Inspiration for
A Choral Group

A.C. Williams Jr. graduated in 1938 from Tennessee State University, formerly Tennessee Agricultural & Industrial State College. A land-grant institution for "Negroes," the college received university status in September 1951. It was created after the passage of the Morrill Land-Grant College Act of 1862.

In those days, Black students desiring to teach school opted to attend a college or university. With his college days behind him, Williams took a job teaching at a "dormitory high school for Black children" in Whiteville, Tennessee.

"We stayed on campus there (where animals roamed)," Joan Elizabeth Patterson, who was three or four years old then, recalled. "I got lost, and everybody on campus was wondering where I was. Apparently, they had a chicken coop. When they found me, I was in the chicken coop with the hens."

The flashback induced a smile and a light chuckle from Patterson, Williams's daughter. Reminiscing about her father and their relationship also brought joy to her heart.

Patterson and her father were inextricably linked together, to say the least. She was there — had always been there — even when he was beginning his teaching career and thereafter. Teaching, for the most part, was a calling for Williams and he pursued it with passion and a readiness for the sake of the children.

Williams landed a job at Manassas High School teaching tenth-grade biology. Manassas is steeped in history and one of the oldest schools in Memphis and Shelby County for Black students. Booker T. Washington High School, Williams's alma mater, is the other.

Manassas was established in 1899 on the west side of Manassas Street. The school originally began as a two-room framed structure in 1900. A Rosenwald School, it was one of the largest schools in the county school system. Improvements were made to the school throughout the years.

Rosenwald Schools were funded in 1917 in part by Julius Rosenwald, a friend of the legendary Booker T. Washington, who was heralded as a great educator, orator, author, and advisor to U.S. presidents.

Rosenwald was co-owner and president of Sears Roebuck and Company and a philanthropist who donated millions to the construction of schools primarily for African Americans in poor, disadvantaged, rural areas across the Southern states.

It was Booker T. Washington who encouraged Rosenwald to address the plight of education for African-

American children in the U.S. The door to an education was now opened to Black disadvantaged children.

Booker T. Washington High School in Memphis began as the Clay Street School in 1873. It was renamed Kortrecht High School in 1891 and renamed again in honor of Washington in 1926.

In a sense, the two schools — B.T.W. and Manassas — would become ground zero for a slate of young talented African-American students, whom Williams assembled at Manassas High School for his newly minted choral group: The Teen Town Singers.

The idea for The Teen Town Singers was spawned in 1945 after Williams had organized a boys' glee club to work as an ensemble in an annual school show at Manassas. Williams, teaching biology at that time, had written and produced the show at Ellis Auditorium that year.

The historic Ellis Auditorium opened its doors in October 1924 in downtown Memphis at the corner of Poplar Avenue and Main Street. It was razed in 1999 and replaced with the Cannon Performing Arts Center.

In its heyday, the multipurpose auditorium served as a venue for concerts, wrestling, a dance hall, and more. A Confederate veterans convention was held there too. Now, Williams was using it for his school show.

Williams derived inspiration for the choral group of high school students after listening to a white choral group over the radio called "Young America Sings."

"They came on every week, and Daddy wanted a similar thing for Black kids," Patterson said. "He thought that Black Americans should have their own glee club."

The harmonious voices that Williams heard each Saturday afternoon from WMC's Goodwyn Institute Auditorium studio belonged to a youthful group of boys and girls from various backgrounds that WMC and *The Commercial Appeal* station had assembled. Directed by John Hyde Cleghorn (aka Uncle Johnny), "Young America Sings" was considered one of the most popular radio programs in the Mid-South.

Originally known as the WMC Talent Foundation, the group was founded in January 1939 to give young boys and girls an opportunity to be heard before an audience while they were being offered "free musical guidance for inherent abilities." There were roughly 90 members in the group. A WMC orchestra accompanied them during broadcasts.

Auditions were held for boys and girls no more than fifteen years of age once a week at WMC studios after school hours. The process was "simple" yet "rigid." The group sang "current hits, hits of yesterday, standard favorites, light opera arias and hymns."

Now geared up to sell his own idea of a choral group — this time with Black students from inner-city high schools — Williams approached a Wilson Mount in 1947. Mount was the music supervisor and later the program director at WMC-TV Channel 5. He counseled, advised, and even tried to get a couple of radio stations in Memphis interested. They weren't buying.

It wasn't until 1949 that Williams was fortunate to get a nod from WDIA after the radio station switched to an all-Black format and on-air personalities. According to Williams, who left handwritten notes on the birth of The Teen Town Singers, "In that year, WDIA was already pioneering in Negro programming, and owner/manager Bert Ferguson approached several people with the same idea in his mind."

Was it fate or God's will that WDIA would become the springboard that Williams would need to launch his young, talented Teen Town Singers across the station's airwaves? Perhaps it was both, considering Williams's abiding faith in God and his deep roots in the Christian church.

Although similar ideas were discussed, Williams was called in and offered another type of show while a Matt Garrett was asked if he was interested in producing a live glee club show with WDIA. According to Williams, Garrett turned the offer down.

Garrett's refusal to produce a glee club show at the behest of WDIA presented a real opportunity for Williams, who approached Ferguson to tell him about his four-year-old dream. Ferguson was sold on the idea and gave Williams the green light to proceed.

With his dream now about to materialize, Williams spent the next four weeks organizing The Teen Town Singers and readying them for their big debut on WDIA. To sharpen their vocal skills, the teens had to undergo rigorous practice sessions weekly.

The Teen Town Singers were now ready for the big day. They were ready to test their mettle, to prove their worth, to affirm their purpose. On Saturday, June 11, 1949, at 4 p.m., their maiden voyage began and was recorded into the annals of radio history. Williams served as narrator and director. William Thaw Jones, his assistant director and former music instructor at Douglass High School, played the piano.

The Teen Town Singers sang the following numbers to the delight of the listening audience: "Blue Skies," "Trees," "Good News," "Every Time I Feel the Spirit," "Bewildered (by a Quartet)," "Moonglow," and "St. Louis Blues." The experience was new to them, in terms of performing on radio, and they looked forward to returning each Saturday for an encore.

The blended voices of The Teen Town Singers reverberated through the airwaves at WDIA and fell on listening ears. Their practice sessions during the week had prepared them for an experience that The Teen Town Singers couldn't possibly phantom. They were convicted and convinced now that they could achieve almost anything.

Williams had given them purpose, a sense of direction, a voice to express themselves collectively and individually, and a reason to complete their journey of choral development and self-discovery.

"It was some of the best years of our lives," said Dr. Ada Shotwell, recounting her experience with The Teen

Town Singers.

"It was wonderful," Joy Harvey Plunkett added.

James Nolan felt the same way, but then offered this point: "You had to be committed, you know, something to hang your hat on."

The original Teen Town Singers were Charles Smith, a Tennessee State University alum; Bernice West, who became a teacher; Thomas Doggett, a band director at Hamilton High School; George Koen, who pursued classical music; Booker T. James, a social worker; Jean Farrow, a teacher; Webster Williamson, also a teacher; James E. Swearingen, a teacher and judge; Mildred Cash, a secretary; Allyene Coleman, a teacher; Norma Jean Ford, a teacher as well; Tearched Scott, a postal worker in Chicago; Gloria Braxton, a lab technician; Norma Grandberry, a teacher; Gloria Harris, also a teacher; and Robert Thomas, a disc jockey at WDIA. The others were Charles Johnson, Fannie Jones, Jesse Neely, Willie Williamson, Eddie Wortes, and William Thaw Jones.

7

'He Was My Superman'

Joan Elizabeth Patterson

When **Joan Elizabeth Patterson** was growing up under the watchful eyes of her parents — Joan Herrisse Romby Williams and Andrew Charles "A.C." Williams Jr. — she was reluctant to tell anyone she would meet that her father was the reputed radio personality setting the airwaves ablaze at WDIA AM-1070, the city's preeminent radio station for the Black listening audience. She would remain mum on the subject, even though the radio listening audience and the community at large had held her father in high esteem.

"I wouldn't tell them that my father was A.C. Williams," said Patterson, who was young and trying to assert her independence and hoping to carve out a path in life for herself. "They had goals for me. Therefore, I tried to achieve those goals rather than everybody knowing who my father was."

Patterson, however, had her own ideas and never felt left out or ignored. Williams had a nickname for his little girl. He called her "Princess." Even though she was doing her own thing to build her own identity and forge her own path, "he was taking care of me. He was just a wonderful man. He was a good father. And he always made me feel like I *was* his princess."

In the Williams household, acquiring a good education was germane. It was a worthy pursuit, and A.C. and Joan H. Williams, whom Patterson was named after, wouldn't let their daughter forget it or squander her education. Both of her parents were professionals in their own fields of endeavor, and both were community servants.

Joan H. Williams, formerly Joan Herrisse Romby from Louisiana, was a Girl Scout leader and a contralto opera singer. Williams, on the other hand, was teaching biology at Manassas High School and establishing a career in broadcasting. So, Patterson decided that she would chart a different course in her life altogether and study science rather than hang onto her famous father's coattails to get ahead.

Ironically, Patterson's decision to pursue a career in science was more in tandem with her father's affinity for biology than his penchant for making a name for himself at WDIA, where his commitment to serving the African-American community and its young people was a worthy pursuit that was widely known throughout the Mid-South.

Williams was very influential. "People liked to sit down and talk to him," Patterson said. "Young men would ask him for advice, and the young ladies admired him. He was just one of those kinds of people with such a strong personality.

"He had influenced me a lot when I got to be a senior in high school," said Patterson, graduating in 1956 from Booker T. Washington High School in Memphis. "I was getting ready to go to college — me and MaShavon Brooks. Her father was a preacher, I think. Daddy sat us both down and said, 'You need to go into science. That's where the money is going to be.' I listened. She didn't."

Brooks went on to earn a PhD in English and found employment at a college in Oklahoma, said Patterson, who majored in biology and minored in education in her pursuit of a college degree. After BTW, her college career began after she matriculated at Tennessee State University, her father's alma mater.

Williams majored in agriculture at TSU and was conferred a degree in 1938. After following her father to TSU, Patterson earned a Bachelor of Science degree in 1960 and another Bachelor of Science degree from the University of Tennessee in 1964. "I was one of the first Blacks at UT Med Tech School and was one of the first Blacks to graduate with a BS in Medical Technology," she said.

Patterson had no problem shying away from the spotlight, even at an early age and throughout her college days, rather than trying to walk in her father's footsteps, or duplicate his success as an on-air personality at WDIA. She just wasn't drawn to the hullabaloo, the fanfare, and the uproarious excitement surrounding her father, nor was she attracted to the buzz that his magnetic personality was generating.

He was essentially "Daddy," she said, and a husband and father who was just as doting and focus-driven at home as he was at the radio station and in the community. She was secure in her own skin and wasn't consumed with jealousy because her father was devoting so much time and attention to children in the classroom, at WDIA, and in the community.

"He loved young children," said Patterson, who understood that her love for her father, or his love for her, was never in jeopardy outside the home — even after Williams had become a surrogate father to countless children who likewise called him "Daddy" and held him in high esteem. "I didn't feel I was losing anything because he had so much time for other youngsters. I didn't feel left out."

Williams made sure of that. Afterall, she was his princess. So love flowed endlessly throughout the home, and Patterson didn't mind sharing her father with those who weren't as fortunate to have a father for themselves, or those who had a father but was MIA from the home. As her parents' only child, she had their full attention — even when something went wrong in the house.

"I always felt the love of both of them," she said. "[However], anything that went wrong in the house, the first person they were going to call was me. 'Joan, did you do this?'" So, sharing the love was quite okay with Patterson. "Being the only child, I liked not having the heat on me. So, I was never jealous."

Williams surrounded himself with children, Patterson said, and acquainted himself with their parents as well, at least the parents who had a vested interest in their children.

He also was aware of family dynamics and stood in the gap for the boys and girls who needed a strong father figure.

"It was a lot of fellas and girls who didn't have fathers, and Daddy was a father figure to mostly all of them," Patterson said. "A lot of them didn't know their daddies. In fact, a lot of kids didn't have fathers who paid attention to them or took time with them. Unfortunately, most men didn't like to take responsibility for kids."

You couldn't say that about Williams, who took responsibility for other parents' kids while he was an educator, a radio personality, and a community servant. His first responsibility, however, was to his family: a wife, Joan Williams, who was a standout singer and was good enough to join the professional ranks; and his daughter, who cherished him dearly as long as she could remember.

When Patterson was a little girl, around two, the pompadour hairstyle was very popular in those days. "I wanted my hair like that," she said. "My mom didn't feel like a two-year-old should wear it. [But] Dad wanted to please his little girl. So, he took a shoe spoon and wrapped my hair around it into a pompadour. He wanted me to feel like a little princess. I was his little princess."

The year was 2019 when Patterson recounted a few tidbits about her father — his sterling career, his love of children, and his love for her and vice-versa — to a reporter from *The Tennessee Tribune,* a Black weekly newspaper headquartered in Nashville, Tennessee. The story was riveting. It was a condensed version that allowed readers to peer into the life of one heck of a guy who called himself "Moohah."

"He was my superman," said Patterson. "I thought my father could do anything. [But] I realized he wasn't a perfect person, but he was definitely a good person."

Williams may not have been more powerful than a locomotive or able to leap tall buildings in a single bound, but he was, in Patterson's opinion, a simple man who was just as "mighty."

And playful, too, she added. In the early morning hours around 1 a.m., for example, Patterson said her father would come home hungry after a long day at WDIA and working side jobs at night.

"I guess [he needed] to make extra money sometimes," she said. "He would come home late sometimes around 1 a.m. and he would be hungry. In those days, Culpepper's [Chicken Shack] was hot. Daddy would come home sometimes and he wanted fried chicken. My bedroom was the first one he would get to. He would come in and open the sack under my nose and wake me up. He knew I liked ribs and fried chicken. Then we'd go in the kitchen and eat up a storm."

Patterson said her father's antics were the same when he brought home hamburgers and milkshakes one time from the Harlem House. "Again, he'd come to my room and open the sack and say, 'I guess you don't want a hamburger and milkshake?'" Once again, she would get out of bed and march to the kitchen with her father in the early morning hours to eat hamburgers.

Patterson was enamored with her father. "I liked everything that Daddy liked," she said. "If Daddy liked it, I liked it. Daddy liked chocolate ice-cream, which I love. He would give me some. He loved peach ice-cream. Until this day, I like peach ice-cream."

Williams's early morning eating habits created a special bond between a father and his little "Princess." Although Patterson was often awakened by the aroma of food wafting under her nose, she enjoyed the attention, nevertheless. But there was one food item that Williams would bring home that Patterson doesn't like today: Donuts.

"In those days, the only donuts that you could get were sugar glazed donuts," said Patterson, who was in the first or second grade when the family was living at 861 South Lauderdale. "Daddy would go at five in the morning and get a dozen donuts and come back and wake me up. Then we'd go in the kitchen and eat hot donuts. Now I can't eat them."

They would also make up songs together. "Before we enclosed the back porch at 861 [South Lauderdale], when it was raining really hard, we'd sing our favorite song about rain: "Come on in into the house, good Lordy/Come on in into the house, my God/Come on in into the house, because it's raining outside."

She chuckled and added: "We had a pretty good relationship until I got to be a teenager. I wanted to do things my way and Daddy was strict. He had his rules and he stood by them too. We got along off and on — especially during my Teen Towner days. Me, Momma, and Daddy, we had a little hard time there when I was, you know, trying to grow up and spread my wings."

Her mother would be the one to administer physical punishment, she said. But after the age of nine, she would defer to Williams, who would admonish Patterson, saying in no uncertain terms: "As long as you're staying in this house, you're gonna follow the rules."

8

'I Begged Dad To Let Me Join'

The Teen Town Singers had two things in common: They were young kids from the inner-city schools and understood that A.C. Williams Jr. was the leader of the group. He was their progenitor as well and ran the operation as he saw fit. With Cathryn Rivers Johnson assisting him as the group's pianist, and with the backing of WDIA, the two educators employed their skills to build a class of A-plus youngsters.

Carla Thomas

Surprisingly, **Carla Thomas** was eleven years old when she became a Teen Towner. She was rather young at the time considering that members had to be in high school to participate in the program. Determined to become a member, Thomas found a way. She begged her father — the legendary Rufus Thomas, a disc jockey at WDIA at that time — who was acquainted with several legends at the radio station, including Williams.

"I wasn't supposed to even join until I was fourteen and in the ninth grade. But I begged Dad to let me join. I didn't say take me down to WDIA and then just look at them [Teen Town Singers]. The first time I heard them, it was like the Holy Spirit said, 'You supposed to be in that group.'" Thomas remembered.

Rehearsals were grueling each Wednesday and Friday after school. Plus, The Teen Towners would sing on the radio at WDIA at ten in the morning on Saturdays. Thomas said her mother, Lorene, was certain that she wouldn't have the discipline for such a weekly undertaking and wouldn't last long in the program.

She said her parents didn't even know that she could sing. She didn't either. Instead, she was enamored and just wanted to be a part of this collaborative of up-and-coming singers, whom she would listen to faithfully over the airwaves each Saturday morning. The experience was a delightful one, she said, and one that would nudge her until she succeeded at becoming a bona fide member of the teen group.

Thomas had her mind set; she wasn't budging. It was just that simple. Or was it? "I wasn't even singing," she said, reminding herself that she was a mere ten-year-old aspiring singer at that time. "I was just listening to, you know, to everything that was going on at that radio station. We were just so happy to have a Black radio station."

The Thomas family was inundated with music, she said. Rufus and Lorene Thomas lived in the Foote Homes Housing Project with their three children: Marvell, a musician who joined The Teen Town Singers at twelve after Carla had joined, and Vaneese, the youngest of the siblings, would sing as well — but not in the early days as a Teen Town Singer. Eventually her voice would resonate in the entertainment world.

"My mother, early in the morning, didn't play nothing but country. I had it all. I had the country; I had the R&B; and I had the Blues. [Also], Daddy would take us to the amateur shows," said Thomas, and remembered that her father was spinning records at WDIA as a disc jockey with access to a trove of music while hobnobbing with some of the best-known musicians and entertainers, bar none.

Growing up in a musical household, Thomas was surrounded by her father's famous friends, including Nat D. Williams, who taught history — her father was one of Nat D.'s students — at Booker T. Washington High School. And then, too, Nat D. was a church member of Thomas's at St. John Baptist Church at the intersection of Vance Avenue and South Orleans Street. He was not yet a luminary at WDIA, but he'd proven to be the right fit for an ailing radio station on the fringes of defunction.

The church was Thomas's connection to music as well. It was her spiritual center. She was a member of the children's choir. However, after the age of twelve, she was aged out. With so much music within her sphere of influence, she was ready for a new venture — a slot with The Teen Town Singers.

Thomas wouldn't give up; she continued to plead with her father to let her join the teen group. He relented, she said, and told her he would speak with A. C. Williams.

She said her father discussed what he'd told Williams. "He said, 'Oh, my God! My daughter is so enamored with your show. I don't know what I'm going to do with her. She would almost cry, saying she wants to be a Teen Towner. She ain't but ten years old.'"

According to what her father told her, Williams responded with an emotional reply: "Oh, no, Lord! We got rehearsals Wednesdays and Fridays. No, no, no!"

"They would get together all the time" — Rufus Thomas and A.C. Williams — "and Daddy would say, 'She's begging me again. Her ear is glued to the Teen Towers [on the radio every Saturday].' "I would talk to Daddy the night before. He was on [WDIA] late at night on Fridays. [On] Saturday, I was up early so I could hear them."

After the thirty-minute teen program ended one Saturday, Thomas said Cathryn Johnson, pianist for the Teen Towner Singers, followed the teen program with a show of her own.

"Sometimes the Teen Towners would stick around if somebody didn't show up for her talent show," Thomas said. "She would stick one of them in there or let two or three of them [from Salem Gilfield Baptist Church, where she also played the piano] sing a number."

Johnson needed to fill the spot, Thomas said.

Rufus Thomas soon yielded to his daughter's pleadings, which was reflected in her youthful voice, after she insisted on becoming a member of The Teen Town Singers.

"Would you just like to go and sit and watch them?" Thomas remembered her father saying.

When that day finally arrived, Thomas said her father told her that he had to go to the radio station to pull his show, meaning he had to get the vinyl records together to play them over the airwaves.

Thomas remembered her father telling her, "Martha Jean said she would look after you."

Martha Jean "The Queen" Steinberg joined WDIA in 1954. She was reportedly one of the first female disc jockeys in the United States. She would eventually carve out a successful niche in radio.

"She'd just gotten off the air with [Robert Daniel] 'Honey Boy' [Thomas]," another WDIA luminary, Thomas said. "They had a show together [called Boy Meets Girl]."

Thomas said Steinberg watched her while she watched The Teen Town Singers through a glass petition at the radio station. "They sang. This is how I met the little lady (Cathryn Rivers Johnson) who played for Salem Gilfield," she added.

Thomas finally was able to join the teen group at the age of eleven. Her pleadings paid off. She learned the songs that Williams was teaching with Johnson's assistance on piano.

At this juncture in Thomas's life, the family moved out of the Foote Homes Housing Project into a home on Kerr

Avenue in the vicinity of Hamilton High School, where she'd begun attending classes.

"I was really supposed to be in the ninth grade. That was one of his [Williams] rules," she said. "And the kids had to be self-sufficient. By fourteen, they could get to where they were going and get back. At eleven, they were a little nervous."

Practice sessions were Wednesdays and Fridays. So, the only way to get there was by bus, she said. "Daddy was not there. I came right out of school and caught the bus."

Thomas's voice at that age was perhaps a little mature, defined, and well-cultivated since she was always around musicians and entertainers whom her father had known personally.

And thanks to Williams, she was able to hone her skills on songs she took the lead on — particularly the pop songs, which Williams had assigned to her, and since she was a gifted and budding contralto — and belting them out when The Teen Town Singers performed Saturdays on radio and throughout the community.

From the age of eleven to seventeen, Thomas was indeed a bona fide Teen Town Singer and developed along the way into a fine specimen of a singer under Williams's directions and with Johnson on piano.

It wasn't long before Thomas started singing with her father. She was still a teenager and would follow him down to Beale Street — the entertainment district — and to other venues where he would perform. Then he proposed singing a duet with her and recording it.

The song, Thomas pointed out, was "'Cause I Love You," which caught the attention of record executive and producer Jim Stewart, who, along with his sister Estelle Axton, founded Satellite Records in 1957 and changed the name to Stax Records. The record caught fire and Stewart, Thomas said, asked for more.

She followed the success of "'Cause I Love You" with "Gee Whiz (Look at His Eyes)." The year was 1961. Thomas had written the song when she was seventeen at Hamilton High School. As it turned out, the engaging song was a million-dollar seller for Stax Records.

Thomas then churned out another smash hit with "B-A-B-Y," a soul-stirring cut that left no doubt in the minds of listeners and those in the music industry that this young upstart, who begged her father to join The Teen Town Singers, was now on the precipice of becoming the unmistakable voice of Southern soul music.

Her star was shimmering bright now. She'd been a Teen Town singer from 1952 to 1960 and made inroads into an industry that was often reserved for those who were tested and proven. But then again not many industry executives would put much stock into a young entertainer — unless their gift of singing far outweighed their youth.

Thomas explained to a reporter from *The Commercial Appeal* in 1992 what she'd learned on her way to becoming the "Queen of Memphis Soul," a title that was bestowed upon her by the executives at Stax Records, who noted her reign as the quintessential songbird of the Memphis sound.

"I learned a lot of professionalism," she was quoted as saying. "How to project my voice. Not to be afraid of the microphone." In addition, she "learned to overcome shyness" and to develop "a whole sense of definition for my style."

Without mentioning his name in the newspaper story, it wouldn't have been a surprise, or one wouldn't be too presumptuous, if Thomas was referring to Williams, who worked intensely with his Teen Town Singers as if they were indeed being trained as a feeder group for Stax Records, or for any record label throughout the industry looking for raw talent.

Thomas had become a breakout artist at such a tender age. She utilized what she'd learned as a Teen Town Singer under Williams and multiplied it ten-fold.

9

'He Instilled Christian Values In Us'

I would say that A.C. disciplined us," said **Cheryl Fanion Cotton**, who remembered Williams "bending some of those guys over those school chairs that we sat in...he didn't touch the girls...and paddling them. I was scared to death quite frankly."

Like the other students that Williams worked with, Cotton concluded that the man who took any number of kids under his wings was just as tough as he was tender-hearted.

Cheryl Fanion
Cotton

"The rest of us were sitting there saying, 'I'm gonna do everything I can to make sure that Mr. Williams never even had to chastise us,'" said Cotton, whose respect and admiration for Williams was unparallel.

"Mr. Williams really raised us. He was an incredible human being. One of the finest you could ever meet. He was just a blessing," she said.

Before Cotton learned that Williams was strait-laced, it was suggested by Cathryn Rivers Johnson that Cotton might want to join The Teen Town Singers. Johnson played piano and taught at Booker T. Washington High School, where Cotton sang in the school choir.

"We used to rehearse in the music room at BTW," said Cotton, who likewise adored and respected Johnson, one of her teachers and the school choir director. "She suggested that I might want to join The Teen Town Singers. So that's what I did."

A resident of South Memphis, Cotton was in nineth grade at BTW when she joined Williams's teen program at the behest of Johnson. She spent three years in the program and graduated at seventeen in 1968 with a $500 scholarship.

Williams had doled out scholarships to his Teen Town Singers who were college-bound and Cotton had earned one. "I received one of the top scholarships," she said proudly.

Because Cotton's father, Gerald Fanion, was involved in the civil rights movement, it may have been a natural tendency for her to join him. "I was very active in the sanitation strike. My dad was too," she said.

"We'd go to the marches. He knew everybody and never met a stranger," said Cotton, including Roman Catholic nuns, whom she was introduced to by her father. "He said, 'Cheryl, why don't you march with them.' He didn't want me out there by myself."

The nuns awarded Cotton a $500 scholarship for college as well. With the Teen Town scholarship and the scholarship that she received from the nuns, "I did my first year at Siena College," she said.

Siena College was established by Dominican nuns in 1922 on the grounds of St. Agnes Academy at Vance and Orleans in Memphis, Tennessee, before the private Catholic college moved to Poplar Avenue just east of Cherry in 1953. The all-female college closed in 1972.

After Cotton's stint at Siena College, she was accepted to the University of Pittsburgh in January of 1970 and graduated in 1973. Then she attended the school of theology at Boston University in 1974, Pittsburgh Theological Seminary from 1975 to 1978, and earned a Master of Divinity from Memphis Theological Seminary in 2000.

Cotton grew up in a home in South Memphis at 561 Edith Avenue. She attended Centenary United Methodist Church, where the Reverend James "Jim" Lawson was her pastor who summoned Dr. Martin Luther King Jr.'s help with the burgeoning sanitation strike.

"I lived across the street from Maxine Smith. And Maxine knew that I was a Teen Town Singer," Cotton said. "She would invite me to meet with her when we had the mass meetings at Clayborn Temple or Mason Temple. She would let me get the crowd fired up by singing the different freedom songs."

Though Cotton was heavily involved in the movement,

she never forgot her roots as a Teen Town Singer. She sang throughout West Pennsylvania and traveled extensively, even across the globe on a safari in Africa, for instance, traveling some 3,000 miles.

"One thing that A.C. Williams taught us...he instilled Christian values in us," she said.

A retired Memphis City Schools teacher and a GED (General Education Development Test) instructor for nearly 30 years, Cotton said it is the teacher's responsibility to fill in some of the parental needs of children.

"I think that is what A.C. did," she said.

As a tribute to Williams, she added: "Everywhere I've gone in my life, I've told people about A.C. Williams. All my friends in Pittsburgh knew about The Teen Town Singers. Wherever I lived all over Mississippi...

"There are two people that I always talked about, because I feel like they are mentors and role models to me. One is A.C. Williams and the other is Jim Lawson."

10

'Mr. Williams Made Me A Member'

It could be described as happenstance or perhaps good luck that **Gwendolyn Quirley** would find herself a bona fide member of The Teen Town Singers before she enrolled in the ninth grade at Manassas High School, where A.C. Williams, the founder and director, taught biology.

Gwendolyn
Quirley

Whether it was "happenstance" or "good luck," "Mr. Williams made me a member," said Quirley, who had no idea that she would be accepted as a Teen Town Singer the day she followed her sister, Aretha Yvonne Townsel, to a Teen Town rehearsal.

"My sister was a Teen Town Singer, and I used to go visiting with her," said Quirley, a little more than two years younger than her sister, who graduated from Manassas as well. "She had me going to rehearsals with her for company. I didn't go initially to join."

Quirley lived in the North Memphis community near

Grant Elementary School, where she had been a student, and in walking distance from St. Joseph Hospital, the current site of St. Jude Children's Research Hospital.

"I started in the summer of 1958 leading up to my ninth grade," she said, but quickly added that it was a prerequisite for a student to be in the ninth grade to participate in the teen program.

"I was at Grant from the first through the eighth grade. I joined the group before I got to Manassas," explained Quirley, one of John H. Townsel and Mildred Townsel's six children.

Quirley sang soprano. She honed her voice in the church choir at Cummings Street Baptist Church in her youth when the church was located on Jackson Avenue in North Memphis and before the congregation moved to Winchester Road in the Whitehaven community.

"I've been there [a member of Cummings] all my life. I've never been a soloist. I was a backgrounder," said Quirley, whose parents were married at Cummings in 1922 when the church was located on Jackson Avenue.

Quirley said she enjoyed singing with The Teen Town Singers but stressed that she didn't have the voice to take the lead. Instead, the comradery and the relationships that she forged with Williams and her fellow choral mates were just as enjoyable.

"It gave us a chance to meet other children from other schools because it was geared to children at all schools," she said. "We were able to attend the Goodwill Revue and the Starlite Revue too."

Quirley recalled the day the teens were practicing on songs they were scheduled to sing at one of the revues. "He wanted your eyes on him," she said. "There was noise in the hallway and I happened to turn my head. He told me to go out there and stay out there. I didn't know he was looking at me at that particular point."

Williams also was a stickler for being on time, she said, a fact that was confirmed by her choral mates. "He was sterned. He didn't play. If we got there late, he would say, 'You might as well turn around and go back home.'"

Quirley said her parents didn't play either. So she was used to following the directives and the rules of a disciplinarian. "During that time a lot of our parents were disciplinarians anyway," she said. But then there was another side to Williams that still warms her heart: He was a surrogate father and "treated all of us the same."

"A lot of times we would wait to catch the bus to go to the radio station and he would pass us [sic] by with a carload already. It would be two or three of us out there [at the bus stop] and he would put all of us in the car. He was just that type of person. I just loved him. He was Daddy; that's the way we took it.

"He believed in education," she continued. "He wanted to make sure our report cards were up to par. He would check our report cards. He wasn't just a director; he was definitely Daddy to us. We were all sisters and brothers. Even now, we call ourselves sisters and brothers.

That's the way we were brought up."

If Quirley learned anything from Williams and being a member of The Teen Town Singers, it would be discipline. "He taught us discipline. He had a big influence on me," she said. "He helped me to learn different things. How to carry yourself. You didn't go in there dressed any kind of way. He and Cathryn Johnson took time with us."

She said Williams and Johnson, the pianist for The Teen Town Singers, whom she affectionately called "Momma," became a part of her family tree.

"When the young ladies had problems, they were our parents. If it was something that they had to talk to our parents about, they did that. There were some who had problems, and he [Williams] made sure they were taken care of. He was a daddy. That's what we called him."

Being a member of The Teen Town Singers "was very beneficial to me," said Quirley. Although she preferred to sing in the background, she pointed out that Williams and Johnson encouraged young singers to face their fears if they were hampered to speak or sing.

Quirley spent five years with Williams and the choral group. She graduated from Manassas in 1963 and received a small scholarship to attend LeMoyne College.

"I didn't go to college right after school," she said. "I went to Pepperdine University (in California) for a couple of years and got a certificate in IT (Information Technology).

She also studied at a few trade schools. "I hate I didn't finish college like some of the others. But I don't think I did too bad." Her IT skills — in addition to her skill set in data entry — were put to good use as a supervisor and manager in the IT department at the former Regional Medical Center of Memphis (The MED).

"I didn't really retire," said Quirley, who was 54 years old then. "They went into reduction."

Later, she found a job at Orgill, Inc. in the credit department. "I am doing some of the same things that I was doing at The MED," said Quirley, the mother of one child, Annazette Quirley, who died nearly 10 years ago.

Quirley has a grandson and three great grandchildren whom she is quite fond of; they bring her joy. Her grandson, she said, is very much aware of her legacy with The Teen Town Singers.

"Oh, yes!" she exclaimed. "My daughter was too. As a matter of fact, she got a chance to meet Mr. Williams. We did a lot of photography and video. One time we interviewed him."

11

'Everybody Knew The Teen Town Singers'

What **Moses Peace** remembers about The Teen Town Singers were the outings where he and his choral mates would stand before an audience and sing their hearts out. The Starlite Revue and The Goodwill Revue were two examples that opened Peace's eyes to a whole new world where he could woo the audience with his melodious bass voice.

"It was the most exciting thing that I've ever done," he said, sounding a bit giddy when he was asked to share his experiences at both signature events for WDIA and with A.C. Williams, director of The Teen Town Singers and the radio station's announcer and director of community relations.

"We backed Rufus Thomas," he recalled while reflecting on the memories that never faded over time, except he couldn't remember any other superstar singer or entertainer that The Teen Town Singers were privileged to sing back up on the big stage.

But then he was quick to acknowledge that "everybody

knew The Teen Town Singers."

They were young high school kids from the inner-city of Memphis who followed Williams's lead, whether they were singing at WDIA on Saturday mornings or in the community at various venues. As their director — and "Daddy" to some of them — Williams tried to instill in them a sense of purpose and belief that they could lasso a shooting star and rise to the top of the world.

"Oh, yes! He was Daddy," he confirmed what others had said about Williams as a father figure, and added: "Didn't nobody talk back to A.C. Everybody respected him."

Peace was impressionable and eager to join the choral group; his brother, Samuel Peace Jr., was already a member. "I guess I just got the bug," he said, and chuckled. But then he added that his passion for singing didn't manifest after his brother had joined the group. It was first developed, he said, at Father Bertrand High School, where he graduated in 1968.

He'd been a Teen Town Singer all during high school — from the tenth grade to the twelfth grade. Like some of the other singers in the group, Peace had to catch a bus to get to practice on Wednesdays and Fridays at the Abe Scharff Branch YMCA, 254 S. Lauderdale Street and Linden Avenue.

"I caught the 4 Walker Alcy," he remembered.

Peace grew up in Lakeview Gardens, the first African American suburban enclave of more than 600 single-family homes that was developed by his father, the Reverend Samuel Morris Peace Sr., who, with his wife Maggie Lynom Peace, had six children. Three are deceased, including Peace's brother, Samuel Peace Jr.

After high school, Peace went to Kemper Military School and College in Boonville, Missouri. He studied business. Then he came back to study at LeMoyne College. He was six hours short from graduating, he said.

Peace still sings. "Only when they ask me," he said.

12

'He Was The Ultimate Teacher, Director'

For **Bernice Smith Brandon**, singing with The Teen Town Singers was an "awesome" experience. "We had fun when it was time to have fun. When it was time to practice, we practiced. When it was time to perform, we performed."

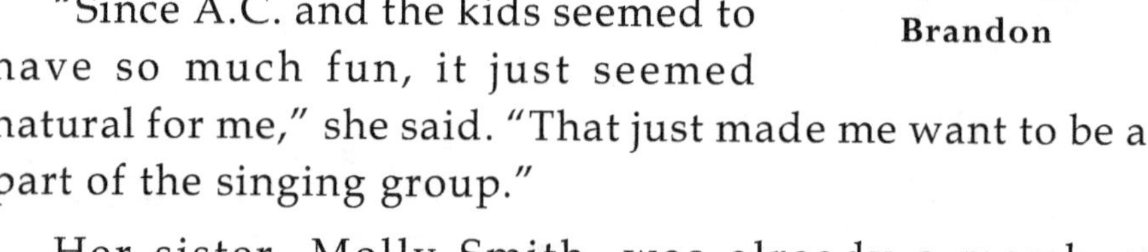

Bernice Smith
Brandon

Brandon loved to sing. She used to listen to The Teen Town Singers belt out songs each Saturday morning over the airwaves at WDIA and envisioned herself being there.

"Since A.C. and the kids seemed to have so much fun, it just seemed natural for me," she said. "That just made me want to be a part of the singing group."

Her sister, Molly Smith, was already a member. Brandon, on the other hand, would join the group during the summer after finishing the eighth grade at Porter Junior High School.

"You were supposed to wait until you were in the ninth grade," said Brandon, and would go on to the ninth grade at Booker T. Washington High School.

At BTW, she sang in Cathryn Rivers Johnson's St. Cecilia Glee Club and in the church choir at Pilgrim Rest Baptist Church when the church was located on Kennedy Street. Sometime later the church relocated to McLemore Avenue, its current location.

"Ms. Cathryn was such a wonderful spirit," she said.

Brandon and her sister Molly lived in the Riverside sub-division between Third Street and Riverside Drive. Her friends, school chums, and Teen Town Singers Glenda Faye Mitchell and Barbara Griffin Winfield lived in the same neighborhood.

Their parents — Willie Mae Smith Gray (mother) and Tommy Cal Smith (father) — had given their blessings for Brandon, the fourth of five children, to join the group. Molly is the third child.

"We were singers," said Brandon, who sang soprano with the Teen Towners.

The group traveled to different high schools and sang during assemblies and other programs. "We might have been the only group in the city that did that," she said.

They also sang at the WDIA Starlite Revue and the WDIA Goodwill Revue. "We sang at the Starlite Revue with the stars of the time, like B.B. King," she said. "We sang in the Goodwill Revue, too, and that was just awesome."

The Starlite Revue, an annual gospel and blues charity concert, was held at Martin Stadium, a baseball park for the home team of the Memphis Red Sox, a Negro League baseball team.

The Goodwill Revue was held at Ellis Auditorium in Downtown Memphis. "We were high school students singing in the [Ellis] auditorium," Brandon said.

Brandon graduated from BTW in 1960. She received a scholarship from The Teen Town Singers like many of the others heading to college. With her scholarship in hand, she matriculated at the University of Arkansas at Pine Bluff, formerly the Arkansas Agricultural, Mechanical & Normal College (Arkansas AM&N). Her major was science and physical education.

After graduating from the university in 1964, Brandon left for Chicago during the Thanksgiving holiday that year. She soon got a job in the Chicago Public School District teaching at Dr. Martin Luther King Jr. College Preparatory High School, where she taught science and physical education.

In addition to her teaching duties, Brandon took the time to coach softball. She was also an assistant volleyball coach and oversaw the cheerleading squad the whole time she was teaching.

Brandon taught at the same school for 35 years and retired. "I enjoyed my profession as a classroom teacher," she said, and was one of thirteen educators to remain with the school since its inception.

Attending church is an integral part of her life as well. After touching down in Chicago, she joined Mt. Calvary Baptist Church at 1259 West 111th Street. "I've been a member since I came to Chicago," she said.

Brandon doesn't sing anymore. At 82, she's taking it easy and enjoying her life in Chicago, where she's lived since finishing college. Her sister Molly Smith also lives in Chicago.

Their mother, Willie Mae Smith Gray, is 103. A niece of theirs, Rosalyn Jackson, is her caretaker. At least once or twice a month, Brandon said she will return to Memphis to relieve Jackson for a week or so.

Her husband died in 2021; they were married 57 years. She has one son. Of all that Brandon has been able to accomplish throughout her life, she credits A.C. Williams and The Teen Town Singers for making it possible to utilize her gift of song and for teaching her the rudiments of a better life.

"You learned patience, respect, and kindness," she said, recalling Williams's teaching. "You start learning that at home. Then you go to school and get that same thing. But A.C. was a reinforcer of all those things.

"If you get that every time you turn around, that will help you in your life with your friendships, your accomplishments as you go, whether you go to college or into the work world.

"Those things that he reinforced in our lives only made us better. It made me want to participate in everything that I was a part of. When I started working, I started using the same type of attitudes and impressions that I learned at home, at school, at church, and with the Teen Towners."

Brandon said The Teen Town Singers was made for young people and called Williams "awesome" for cultivating the lives of so many teenagers. "He was such a giant of a man," she said. "Even though he was tall, his personality was bigger than his statue. He was the ultimate teacher, director."

The teen program had a good run — lasting 21 years. It was disbanded in 1970. "Nothing goes on forever," said Brandon. "But that was one thing that should've lasted in Memphis. But, of course, he [Williams] couldn't last."

Some things you just can't duplicate, she said. "God gives you an ending. You just have a space in time. And I'm so privileged to be a part of that time. It was just wonderful."

13

'We Just Had So Much Respect For Him.'

Juanita B. Mitchum had a choice to make. She could attend Manassas High School or Douglas High School after finishing the eighth grade at Hyde Park Elementary School. "I was on the borderline to go to Manassas or Douglas, I chose Douglas," she said, and graduated in 1958.

Juanita B. Mitchum

Mitchum lived in the Hyde Park community. Her mother was named Marguerite Conway. Her father was James Arthur Blake. She had one brother.

"My parents divorced early in my life," said Mitchum, who would soon meet a man whom she would love and respect — a man who loved children and filled a void for some of them who didn't have a father in the home. That man was A.C. Williams, director of The Teen Town Singers.

"I used to just hear them on the radio [at WDIA] and then I remembered at some point Mr. A.C. Williams would say, 'If you're interested in learning how to sing, we have openings for you.'"

Mitchum was interested in joining the group, but she was only in the eighth grade at Hyde Park Elementary School and would soon pass to the nineth grade at Douglas, her school of choice. One of the rules for joining The Teen Town Singers was that a student had to be in the ninth grade.

There were exceptions. Mitchum was one of them.

"When I went there, I hadn't even gotten into high school," she said. "I was in the eighth grade. But he let me be in there — although it was for high school students. I appeared there one day and he accepted me."

At that time, the Teen Towners were practicing at Manassas High School, where Williams was teaching biology. "Manassas wasn't that far from me," she said, "although I had to ride the bus there. Then they moved to the YMCA on Lauderdale and Linden."

Either way, Mitchum had to catch a bus.

"Sometimes I wouldn't have money to go to rehearsals, 'cause, you know, I had to ride the bus," she said, and added: "I don't care how long I missed and showed up again, he [Williams] always welcomed me. He didn't make me feel like, 'Ahh you get out of here and don't come back.'"

Mitchum said Williams was extra kind to her. But there was one thing about him that she will never forget. "I was always a little skinny, tall girl," she said. "One day I got to the practice before he got there. I was sort of doing something...I guess trying to look short or get short.

"He came to me and said, 'Baby, you're a pretty, little girl and it's nothing wrong with you being tall.' He said, 'You just stand up and stand tall, walk tall, and be tall. You can't do anything about it. You can't make yourself [shorter], but you can make yourself look ridiculous.' He said, 'So straighten yourself up and go on about your business.'"

Mitchum said Williams's encouraging words have stuck with her all these years. "I think this is one thing that kept me in it and kept me motivated," she said, "because of his kindness."

In addition to Williams's kind words and his love of children, Mitchum said she joined The Teen Town Singers because she was interested in "clean, fun-kind of activities."

Was singing her forte? "Not really," she admitted. "I just enjoyed the group. I enjoyed being in it with a lot of different high school students. At that time, we had representation from every high school. I enjoyed meeting and socializing with the other students from the other schools."

Mitchum was recognized as a high school senior class superlative at Douglas. "I was elected the most friendliest," she said proudly. "So, I just like people, being around people. I like mingling, socializing, and getting to know different people."

Being a Teen Town Singer was special to Mitchum in

more ways than one. She enjoyed the comradery, Wiliams's fatherly love, and the outings. "I enjoyed it," she said, "because I got to go to some places with the Teen Towners that I wouldn't ordinarily have gotten a chance to go to."

After graduating from Douglas High School, Mitchum, with a $200 scholarship in hand, opted to study home economics at Tennessee State University. "At that time, if you lived off campus, it was $45 a quarter. So that $200 went a long way with me."

After college, she taught home economics at Wooddale, Manassas, and Kingsbury High Schools. She was certified in fashion design at University of Tennessee at Martin and went on to teach fashion design at Trezevant Career and Technology Center, where she retired after eleven years in the classroom.

Mitchum noted that being a member of The Teen Town Singers and spending time with Williams was unforgettable. Could another group of teenagers find success with an affable leader be duplicated today?

"If they get the right kind of leader, the kind like A.C. Williams," she said. "He motivated us. We just had so much respect for him. We knew better than to do something crazy — even if we weren't in his presence."

She said a choral group like The Teen Town Singers could be useful and helpful to young people today. "It would be something for the students to look forward to after school."

14

'We Were Always One Community'

I remember the first time I ever walked into that rehearsal room," said **Georgia Bland Gleese**, reminiscing about her experience as a Teen Town Singer. "It was like you had status and you were associated with WDIA."

Georgia Bland
Gleese

Status followed Gleese everywhere she went — even at Douglass High School and among her peers in the Hyde Park community, where her father was a community activist and where she lived and attended Hyde Park Elementary.

"That's the way they treated you in school," said Gleese, who basked in the glory of being a valued member of A.C. Williams's prominent choral group. "They treated me like a celebrity in the neighborhood and in church...everywhere."

Gleese was thirteen and passing to the nineth grade at Douglass when she joined The Teen Town Singers. Permission was granted by her father, Joe Bland, and accepted by Williams, whose reputation in the community and at WDIA was widely known.

She remembered their chance encounter — Williams and her father. It was at her father's barbershop at Chelsea and Springdale in Hyde Park. "Mr. Williams was in Hyde Park and stopped by Daddy's barbershop to get a haircut. Either a haircut or a shoeshine," she guesstimated.

"Everybody had got[ten] word of who he was. My daddy spoke to him and asked him could I join [the group] because I loved to sing. I was singing everywhere. I would sing in the church. He said yes, I could do it."

Rehearsals were held during the week, said Gleese, and The Teen Town Singers would sing live in the studios at WDIA AM-1070 on Saturday mornings when the radio station was located on Union and on Central.

"It was just a small building," she recalled. "I'm thinking about how all of us were able to fit inside of that small building to record."

School rivalry was in play, even during those days, at sporting events between schools such as Douglass, Manassas, Booker T. Washington, Carver, and other Black schools, but not between The Teen Town Singers who hailed from those schools, said Gleese, adding that comradery was an equalizer.

"We were all housed in that radio station from all different schools, all different people, all different colors, and nobody was treated like they were different," she said. "He didn't teach you different because you were like me. He didn't have favorites. We were always one community.

"Listening to him on the radio, you would think he would be a father figure to everybody. It didn't matter what was going on in this world, whether it was home or school or just life in general, it seemed like you could go to him and chit chat with him and he would somehow work it out.

"He would get involved in your life. You'd forget about your world, whatever was happening. He was not a standoffish celebrity. He was really like a father figure. Really, there are many Teen Town Singers today who referred to him as Daddy."

After graduating from Douglass High School, Gleese received a $50 Teen Town scholarship to attend Bishop College, a historically black college that was founded in Marshall, Texas, in 1881 by the Baptist Home Mission Society. The college moved to Dallas in 1961 and closed in 1988.

She studied music.

When Gleese entered the workforce, she took a job at the Firestone Tire and Rubber Company in North Memphis. The company closed in March of 1983.

"I didn't do the things that my dad wanted me to do. I went a different direction," said Gleese, who had eight brothers and sisters, and went on to teach special education at Memphis City Schools. She retired in 2000.

"I have a sister who is a principal at the special needs

school in Memphis, Avon Lenox High School. I have another sister who taught the blind. So, we all went to special needs."

Gleese is proud to have been a member of Williams's teen program — even decades later in her twilight years.

"I'm a Teen Town singer today," she said. "I can wear my WDIA Teen Town Singers T-shirt today in Walmart and I guarantee you as many as two or three people are going to tap me on my shoulder and say something to me about The Teen Town Singers."

15

'He Exposed Us To A Lot'

Glenda Faye Mitchell vividly remembers the good times when A.C. Williams Jr. exposed The Teen Town Singers to a bevy of superstar entertainers at WDIA's Goodwill Revue and the Starlite Revue when the teens performed at Martin Stadium.

Glenda Faye
Mitchell

The ballpark was owned by W.S. Martin and his brothers at the corner of Iowa Avenue and Lauderdale Street. It was the home of Negro League Baseball and where African-American community events were held.

"He exposed us to entertainers like James Brown and Michael Jackson and Rufus Thomas. He exposed us to a lot being on those different shows every year," she said.

Mitchell was fourteen and in nineth grade at Booker T. Washington High School when she joined the roster of The Teen Town Singers. Her friends and school chums would remember the name Grear, she said. It was her maiden name.

The Grear family lived in South Memphis at 292 Ingle Avenue in a yellow brick home that time did not preserve. Her mother and father, Jerry and Bessie Grear, raised six children in the home.

Before Mitchell's parents permitted her to join the teen group, she first drew inspiration from the bevy of youngsters singing over the airwaves at WDIA. She herself had been singing in the church choir.

"Just knowing that you can be on the radio every Saturday morning was an inspiration for us to get together with our friends," she said. "And when you leave the radio station you can stop and get your donuts and sit in the back of the bus and eat your donuts."

Segregation was the order of the day, she said. Black bus riders had to move to the back.

Transportation was not provided. Mitchell, who was old enough to venture across the city, took a 7 Crosstown bus from South Memphis and transferred to a 4 Walker to get to rehearsals on Wednesdays after school and to the radio station on Union Avenue on Saturdays.

"You couldn't be late," she said. "That was the highlight of our lives. We looked forward to Wednesdays and Saturdays."

Mitchell sang with the choral group for four years and received a scholarship to attend college. "I think it was $100," she said, and opted to attend the former Arkansas Agricultural, Mechanical and Normal College, which is now The University of Arkansas at Pine Bluff (UAPB), a historically black university.

"My parents couldn't afford to send me to college," said Mitchell. "So, the B.T.W. band director and the band director at UAPB got together and that was how I was able to get a scholarship to complete my four years at UAPB.

"So that right there let me know that your teachers were looking out for you if they felt you had potential [and] to make sure that you completed college," she said. "The Teen Towners were the first impression that you can be able to survive just knowing there are others that care about you.

"I was a drum majorette in high school and that's how I got my scholarship in music," she said.

Being a member of Williams's prized teen group lifted the spirits of Mitchell and her choral mates who used what they'd learned and experienced to catapult them into a world of infinite possibilities.

"All the Teen Towners knew what they could be and...were motivated to do those things," she said.

Mitchell taught school for twenty years, worked fifteen years at Southwest Tennessee Community College, and sold World Book Encyclopedias for ten years. She won a car, she said, after selling so many encyclopedias. She also owned her own business for twenty years, "Let's Talk Turkey Barbeque."

"You never get too old to reach your goal," she said.

When Mitchell thinks about the journey — from her

experience as a Teen Town Singer and her life thereafter — A.C. Williams Jr. comes to her mind. "He was the epitome of a father, a brother, a confidante," she said. "He was everything to us. We all looked up to him."

She also added Cathryn Rivers Johnson, the pianist for The Teen Town Singers, to her list of favorite people. They were family, said Mitchell, and noted that Johnson and Williams "were like Mother and Daddy to us."

16

'It Was Just A Pleasure To Be Connected'

George Washington Carver High School in South Memphis was the stumping ground for **Mary Campbell Bohanon**, who was one of A.C. Williams's Teen Town Singers in grades tenth through the twelfth when she was known by her maiden name, Mary Campbell.

Mary Campbell
Bohanon

Born in Memphis, the Bluff City, Bohanon spent time in Buffalo, New York, and returned to the Bluff City where she matriculated at Carver and soon joined The Teen Town Singers.

Singing had been Bohanon's forte, having song in a group at Greater Mt. Pleasant Baptist Church and at other venues. Getting to church wasn't a problem for Bohanon and her brother — for they found comfort in walking together, she said.

"Me and my brother used to walk all the way from the street we lived on to Kentucky Street every Sunday morning and to choir rehearsals," she said. "We would walk and sing and it wouldn't take us anytime to get there."

So, when an insatiable urge to sing prompted Bohanon and a few friends to walk into one of Williams's rehearsals — much like a walk-on athlete trying out for a sport without prior approval — they caught his attention.

"Well at the time, I was interested in singing and I was singing a whole lot," Bohanon recalled. "So, a few of us got together and just went to rehearsal...whatever...and Mr. Williams accepted us."

With permission from her mother, she had taken her brother James Nelson with her to the rehearsal, although he wasn't old enough to be a member of the coveted teen program. He was only in the seventh grade.

"Mr. Williams liked him," she said. "He let James join before he got in the ninth grade. He nicknamed him 'Big Man' because he was little at that time. He got in at the same time as [Robert] 'Honey Boy's' [Thomas] two daughters, Renee Thomas and Cheryl Thomas."

Bohanon said she and James were raised together, even though her mother had other children. "I was raised by old folks," she pointed out. But that didn't stop her from pursuing her goal of singing.

"I led two spiritual songs... 'Ezekiel Saw the Wheel' and one other," said Bohanon, who remembered when The Teen Town Singers held rehearsals at the YMCA.

"We used to sing on the talent show; that came on at

11:00," she said. "After we'd broadcast, we stayed at the station for half an hour...." The Barkays, she added, played a lot in the talent shows and were invited to play at sock hops (a dance for teenagers).

"We rehearsed every Wednesday and Friday after school," Bohanon said. "Mr. Williams did not play. We had respect for him. He didn't have to yell at us. All he had to do was look at us. If we were on the air and someone got out of character, he would have a frown on his face and then they would straighten up. He was the father away from home."

The experience that Bohanon gained as a Teen Town Singer was undeniable and unforgettable. The opportunities were unquestionable and beneficial as well — like when The Teen Town Singers sang at WDIA's star-studded Goodwill Revue and the Starlite Revue.

"I had the opportunity to meet quite a few people because the Teen Towners used to back up different people like Marvin Gaye, The Temptations, and Smokey Robinson and the Miracles when he would sing with his wife Claudette," she said, including, "Howling Wolf, Gene Chandler, you know, a lot of those different Stars."

Bohannon said she really wasn't over the moon about singing with the stars. Why? "I was used to doing it every week at 10 when we'd come on the air and Cathryn River Johnson was our pianist," she said.

"I feel like he [Williams] gave us an opportunity to really be used to some things. You know how some people are not used to doing anything...but I believe Mr.

Williams really gave us the exposure. I did it in church anyway. So, it wasn't anything new to me that I wasn't familiar with.

"I believe it kept a lot of us young people out of trouble and being around the wrong type of people," Bohanon continued. "It added highlights to our life. I feel like I am well respected and I respect other people. It gave us an outlook on life rather than not reaching for something in life, because a lot of young people nowadays are just lost. They don't have any hope or anything to reach for."

Bohanon said she looked up to Williams, Johnson, Theo "Bless My Bones" Wade, Robert "Honey Boy" Thomas, Rufus Thomas, Ford Nelson, and other WDIA luminaries.

"I believe all of them were examples for us," she said. "I give credit to all those men because they really kept us in line. In other words, they respected us and we respected them."

After Bohanon graduated from Carver High School, "Mrs. [Lorene] Thomas, Rufus Thomas's wife, sent me some money for graduation, because she wasn't able to make it to my graduation."

Bohanon said she had a special relationship with Williams and his wife, Attee Williams. "After Mr. Williams died, I would visit her up until she died. I would take her Mother's Day gifts and different things like that. Mr. Williams said, 'I don't know why she is so crazy about you — but she is crazy about you.'"

Bohanon said she enjoyed the connection to Williams

and the recognition that comes with being a member of The Teen Town Singers — even decades later now that she's in her golden years.

Her memories, however, are golden. She recalled singing at a memorial service at First Baptist Church-Broad in Memphis for the victims of an unfortunate traffic accident.

"They had us to come and do a couple of songs at the memorial. Percy Wiggins (a Teen Town Singer) was with us," she said. "He directed my brother and me. He played the piano for us.

"When I got to the church, one lady said to me, 'Miss Bohanon, I didn't know you were a Teen Town Singer. I see you all singing.' I said, Oh, my God!"

Bohanon didn't know the woman had been paying attention to her and that she had been aware of her legacy. "It's not something that I brag about," she said. "It was just a pleasure to be connected."

17

A Pictorial History

IT'S A FAMILY AFFAIR: A.C. Williams Jr. (top middle) stands proudly with his expanded family, including his stepson Willie Wiley (top left), son-in-law Charles Patterson (top right), daughter Joan E. Patterson (right, second row), his wife Attee Williams (middle, third row), and his grandchildren and great grandchildren.

A Pictorial History

TOP Photo: A.C. Williams Jr., Cathryn Rivers Johnson (at the piano), and The Teen Town singers hitting all the right notes in the studios at WDIA.

RIGHT: Williams donning cap and gown following his graduation from Tennessee A&I State University in 1938 with a bachelor's degree in agriculture.

In June 1949, the *Memphis World*, an African American newspaper founded in 1931 in Memphis, announced a new program called "Teen Town Singers," featuring area high school students. It began on a Saturday at 4 p.m. over the airwaves at Radio Station WDIA. It was considered a public service program that was directed by A.C. Williams.

A Pictorial History

Photo by Lewin-Miller

ABOVE: The original 1949 group with A.C. Williams in the rear and surrounded by his teen singers.

WDIA's Robert "Honeyboy" Thomas (right), one of the first members of The Teen Town Singers, and "Jean," Mrs. Honeyboy.

Some members of the original group from 1949 went on to achieve success in various fields of endeavor after their high school graduation, including Gloria Braxton (left), Irby Cox (bottom left), a pianist, and Webster Williamson, a teacher.

A Pictorial History

At the microphone is Frances Burnett, then a disc jockey in Jackson, Tennessee, and a night club artist with the Rhythmaires who sang at the Flame Show Bar in Detroit, Michigan.

William Thaw Jones, a music instructor at Douglass High School, was also the first assistant director and pianist for The Teen Town Singers.

A Pictorial History

1950: Kennedy Veterans Administration

A young B.B. King thrumming his guitar and commanding the stage.

The Spirit of Memphis Quartet, one of the oldest African American gospel groups in the country, performs while a group of youngsters of observe.

A.C. Williams surrounds himself with his young choral group at WDIA between 1951 and 1952.

A.C. Williams considered Mildred Harrington to be one of his most loyal and hardest working Teen Town Singers.

A.C. Williams directs his Teen Town Singers in song in this 1952 snapshot of his choral group. He referred to Thelma Lee Perry as the all-time "Teen Town Baby."

That same year during the summer of 1952, WDIA tapped A.C. Williams to be the radio station's full-time consultant.

A Pictorial History

Nineteen fifty-two was the contract renewal date between Bert Ferguson, president and general manager of WDIA, Dr. J.E. Walker, who co-founded Universal Life Insurance Company in 1923 with A.W. Willis Sr. and M.W. Bonner, and A.C. Williams (right), who stands next to Ben Olive of Universal Life in this photograph. This photograph was taken in 1953.

Teen Towners: A Family to Universal Life Insurance Co.

The Universal Life Insurance Company had been actively involved in the lives of A.C. Williams's Teen Town Singers by providing them with scholarships if they chose to attend college.

A manuscript marked for a Universal Life brochure reads in part: "The Teen Town Singers, a chorus of talented youngsters from Memphis high schools who appear on WDIA every Saturday morning, have celebrated their first anniversary as part of the Universal family..."

"The Teen Towners are like the children you'll find in millions of homes in the eight-state area served by Universal. Universal protects their future, too."

"They will have a home with their families, and education, and a house to live in if the bread-winner's income keeps coming in."

A Pictorial History

The friendship and comradery that The Teen Town Singers enjoyed at the studios of WDIA is apparent here at T.O. Fuller State Park in Memphis in 1953, where swinging is fun. That year, Rodel Sanders was presented a $120 college scholarship. In all, a total of $1,640 scholarships were awarded, including $100 cash awards to Alpheus Fields, John White III, Emery McIver, and Eddie Lee Duncan; and a $50 award to Adolphus McIver. WDIA contributed $100 to the scholarship.

Apparently 1953 was a good year for Lanetha Collins and Alfred Motlow, whom A.C. Williams referred to as "The Gruesome Twosome." He said Collins and Motlow were "two of the greatest voices the group ever had."

A Pictorial History

A.C. Williams hams it up with Cleatrice Berkley (left), Thelma Lee Perry, and Gloria Wheeler, whom he called the "Brain," and referred to this threesome in 1954 as "a real sweet bunch."

On December 9, 1959, Markhum L. Stansbury Sr. was featured in the *Memphis World*, an African American newspaper that was founded in 1931. Known by his friends as "Old Buddy," he is the son of Mrs. Eliza Stansbury.

Stansbury was very active in his days at Booker T. Washington. He was president of his homeroom, business manager of his senior class and the Student Council, business manager of the Student Librarian Association, foreman of the print shop, editor of *The Washingtonian*. He also was on the school's yearbook staff and became the co-editor.

A Pictorial History

Breaking ground for the Goodwill Home for Negro Youth: Juvenile Court Judge Elizabeth McCain (left), Rev. G.W. Golden, Homes Chairman John Parsons, and WDIA's Vice President and General Manager Bert Ferguson. WDIA contributed $40,000 to the fund to "kick off" fundraising campaign.

Joan E. Williams, daughter of A.C. Williams, is a future Teen Town Singer. The year was 1956, and a birthday party was held in her honor. Joan E. Williams would eventually join the choral group and sing with them for six years.

A Pictorial History

On September 1, 1956, seven Teen Town Singers were awarded scholarships that were presented to them by A.C. Williams and Cathryn Rivers Johnson.

Scholarships Totaling $2,500 Awarded to 7 Teen Towners

On September 1, 1956, seven Teen Town Singers from various high schools in the city of Memphis received altogether a total of $2,500 in scholarships to a college of their choice.

The criteria for receiving a scholarship were based on "length of service, talent, loyalty and attendance."

The winners were announced by A.C. Williams, the group's founder and director, and Cathryn Rivers Johnson, pianist.

Winners receiving a $200 cash award were Magnolia Armstrong, Manassas High School; Jennie Lee Hodge, St. Anthony; Robert Hall, Booker T. Washington High School; and Clara Wilson of Douglass High School.

Also, Booker T. Robinson received an all-expense scholarship to Mississippi Vocational College while Shirley Price got a four-year tuition grant to Tennessee State University. James Craigen received an honorable mention award.

In 1956, WDIA Radio Station held its Goodwill Revue at Ellis Auditorium. On this night in December, Elvis Presley, Ray Charles, B.B. King, Rufus Thomas, and other stars performed – including The Teen Town Singers.

A Pictorial History

On this day in 1957, A. C. Williams is surrounded by a group of youngsters on the grounds of WDIA – "50,000 watts of Goodwill."

Photo by Ernest C. Withers

Also in 1957, A.C. Williams, WDIA's consultant and director of The Teen Town Singers, awarded $1,000 in cash scholarships to Doris Turnstall (left), St. Augustine; Claudia Marie Ivy, Douglass High School; and Magnolia Armstrong and Thelma Lemmons, Manassas High School. A. C. Williams looks on proudly.

The year of 1958 couldn't have been any better for this group of Teen Town Singers who proudly display a banner denoting WDIA as the 'Goodwill Station.'

These Teen Towners weren't shy about receiving scholarships to attend a college or university of their choice. Photo by Ernest C. Withers.

The dynamic Frances Burnett began her professional career with The Teen Town Singers, singing soprano with the teen group on WDIA radio station.

After high school, she attended Lane College for two years. Then she started singing in night clubs and guest-starred with bands such as Duke Ellington's. Then she signed with Decca Records. Shortly thereafter, she rose to great heights in the entertainment world and enjoyed the trappings of success. In 1956, she had her own radio show in Jackson, Tennessee: The Frances Burnett Show. "I'll always be a part of you," she wrote to A.C. Williams.

A Pictorial History

A 1959 group shot of A.C. Williams's Teen Town Singers at the front entrance of WDIA-1070 Radio Station and its "50,000 Watts of Goodwill."

The Teen Town Singers Compete for Prize Money

The Teen Town Singers were moving up in 1959, ten years after A.C. Williams founded the choral group. They were the toast of WDIA, their benefactor, and performed at various venues.

On Sunday, September 20, at Avery Chapel A.M.E. Church, Union Protective Life Insurance Company held its 26th anniversary program. The Teen Town Singers sang on program at least five selections at the 3:30 p.m. program.

This was an awards program, per se, featuring contestants Hortense Spillers, 12th grade, Melrose High School; Nellie M. Crigler, 11th grade, Manassas High School; Marilyn Harris, 12th grade, Father Bertrand; Harold Coston, 12th grade, Lester High School; Delores Jordon, 11th grade, Douglass High School; and Alice Morgan, 12th grade, Hamilton High School.

The first-place prize was $200; second-place, $150; and third-place, $75. Two judges were from LeMoyne College. The coordinator was from Tennessee A&I State University.

A Pictorial History

In 1959, the *Tri-State Defender* published this photo of A.C. Williams and seven members of his Teen Town Singers at WDIA in its September 1 issue. The four girls and three boys shared $1,000 in scholarship money. Front row: Glenda Faye Grear (left), who will attend Arkansas AM&N; Ann Kirk, Tennessee A&I State University; Mrs. Grant Parham, standing in for her son, Grant Jr., Los Angeles City College; Claraniece Smith, Arkansas AM&N; and Williams. Back row: John Ray Buntyn (left), LeMoyne College; James Branch, Owen College; and Marvell Thomas, LeMoyne College. During the group's 10-year history, WDIA has awarded $12,000 in scholarships.

Three young people took home ribbons in WDIA's talent search. Cornelius Warren (left), Poplar Bluff, Missouri, won the Classical Division; May Toy Reaves, Saulsberry, Tennessee, won the Spelling Bee; and Barbara Perry, Melrose High School, won the Pop Division.

The Teen Town Singers celebrated their 10th anniversary in 1959, featuring some of their predecessors on program.

The choral group's 10th anniversary celebration featured Marvell Thomas, Carla Thomas and John Buntyn. A.C. Williams is to the right of the trio.

A Pictorial History

In this 1961 photo of A.C. Williams and former members of his Teen Town Singers, WDIA and the Universal Life Insurance Company awarded them $2,050 in scholarships. Seated, from left: Fannie Farmer, Williams, and Joyce Ann Gates. Standing: Jerry Smith (left), Merilee Hughey, Beverly Buntyn, Percy Wiggins, Martha Jones, Ethel Vann, and Charles Kennon. Cathryn Rivers Johnson, the choral group's pianist and instructor at Booker T. Washington High School, is positioned behind Williams.

In 1960, Myrtis Cobb, a senior at Booker T. Washington High School and "Miss Soul," gets a warm welcome from J.H. White (right), president of Mississippi Valley State University, while A.C. Williams looks on. Williams, in fact, escorted Cobb to the campus.

A Pictorial History

A.C. Williams, founder and director of The Teen Town Singers, stands appreciatively with the Universal of Life Insurance Company scholarship winners in this timeless photo from 1959-1960. Markhum L. Stansbury Sr. (left) and Carla Thomas (left of Stansbury) were proud recipients as well as the others. Cathryn Rivers Johnson is third from the right side of this photo. The insurance company is a program sponsor.

Universal Life Awards Scholarships to Five in 1960

The Universal Life Insurance Company awarded scholarships to five deserving Teen Town Singers. The company's slogan was "Prepare Now…and Guarantee Your Future." That's what the program sponsor was doing when it awarded scholarships to Marilyn Harris, Father Bertrand High School, $750; Yvonne Townsel, Manassas High School, $750; Sandra Durrett, Lester High School, $500; Alice M. Morgan, Hamilton High School, $500, including a partial $250 scholarship; and Sandra Bass, Melrose High School, $500.

Each winner had to write an essay that year in 1960 to compete for the coveted scholarship. There were no restrictions to the scholarships; they could choose any college or university.

Universal Life joined WDIA in administering the scholarships.

Several Teen Town Singers Found Success on the Big Stage

Nineteen sixty-one was a pivotal year for some of The Teen Town Singers. Since 1949, the year A.C. Williams founded the choral group, the first group of teens was enjoying rousing success on the big stage before a much wider audience.

Year after year, teens would graduate from high school and receive scholarships to any college of their choice. But then some of them, after leaving the group, were catapulted to regional and national success in the music business and world of entertainment.

For example, Ed Townend, who started singing with the group in 1949, was now recording with Warner Brothers Records and living in Hollywood, California.

Of course, there was Frances Burnett, a 1949-1950 alumna, who recorded for Capitol Records. Sam Fletcher, also a 1949-1950 alumnus, recorded in New York. Then there were the Parrish twins, Loretta and Henrietta. They worked in Hollywood with Johnny Otis, singer, musician, composer, bandleader, and record producer. Booker T. James, also known as B.T., was teaching special needs children at Mitchell High School and recording as well.

Carla Thomas was in seventh grade when she started singing with The Teen Town Singers. The rule was, according to Williams, the teens had to be in the ninth

grade to participate.

After graduating from Hamilton High School, Thomas attended Tennessee A&I State University in Nashville. While still a student, she joined Atlantic Records and rocketed to instant success with "Gee Whiz (Look at His Eyes)." The song became a national hit. She was only 18.

Thomas was now a bona fide recording artist, a rising star, and enjoyed a wave of success with additional hits added to her repertoire. She didn't let her success interrupt her studies at Tennessee State either.

She majored in English.

A Pictorial History

Talent Contests, Awards Banquets, Selected Venues Were Nothing New to Williams's Teen Town Singers

Talent contests and awards banquets were nothing new to The Teen Town Singers and their director, A.C. Williams Jr., who would often serve as master of ceremonies. Throughout the history of the choral group, their talent and penchant for singing would be on display and reverberate at banquets, other venues, and the Memphis Area Science Fair on May 19, 1961, for example, when they were on program to sing, while three of their choral mates were awarded scholarships: 1st place, Joyce Gates from Carver High School, $600; 2nd place, Marsha Jones of Booker T. Washington High School, $400; and 3rd place, Jerry Smith of Mitchell High School, $250.

Five years earlier, on April 24, 1956, Williams and his choral group were on program with noted concert pianist Lois Towles, whom Tennessee A. and I. State University (now Tennessee State University) presented at Ellis Auditorium. She was a member of the music faculties at TSU and Fisk University, both in Nashville. Again, Williams served as master of ceremonies.

Williams kept his Teen Town Singers busy by showing off their skills to a wide audience — via radio or on stage. There was a Teen Town popularity contest as well in the early '60s. Contest winners were announced in the Teen Town Bulletin.

They were Ann Kirk, *Most Pleasing Personality*; Gloria Massey, *Girl Most Likely to Succeed*; Spencer Wiggins, *Boy Most Likely to Succeed*; Barbara Griffin, *Most Popular Girl*; Clifford Shelby, *Most Popular Boy*; Markhum L. Stansbury Sr., *Most Businesslike Boy*; Bernice Smith, *Most Cheerful Girl*; William Wilks, *Most Cheerful Boy*; Dardeen Woods, *Most Attractive Girl*; James Branch, *Most Attractive Boy*; Eugene McClarin, *Neatest Boy*; Claraneice Smith, *Neatest Girl*; Carroll McSwain, *Most Helpful Boy*; Clementine Cole, *Most Helpful Girl*; John Ray Buntyn, *Most Likeable Boy*; Gwen Edwards, *Most Likeable Girl*; Mary Jean Cooper, *Studious Girl*; Freddie Grant, *Studious Boy*; Carla Thomas, *Talented Girl*; Marvell Thomas, *Talented Boy*; Edwin Brooks, *Most Gentleman-like*; Mayoline Williams, *Most Lady-like*; Isaac Cragien, *Best Boy Comedian*; Carol Willis, *Best Girl Comedian*; Jeanette Wallace, *Dignified Girl*; and Billy Williams, *Dignified Boy*.

A Pictorial History

Several businesses were sponsors of A.C. Williams's (left) Teen Town Singers on WDIA, including the Kroger Company, whose representative announced the teens who were awarded scholarships from the company

Timothy McGuire attended Manassas High School in grades 9-11 and later graduated from Booker T. Washington High School after returning to Memphis from a one-year stint in Detroit. Here, he proudly dons his cap and gown, and would go on to become a successful businessman and entrepreneur.

A Pictorial History

A.C. Williams (Standing: fifth person from left) and Cathryn Rivers Johnson (Seated: third from left) pose with the Teen Town scholarship winners.

After her five-year stint with The Teen Town Singers, Regina Bennett-West would go on to make a pivotal move to rhythm, blues, and gospel, including an oversees junket with The Platters.

Melva Houston, a former Teen Town Singer, autographed this photo for A.C. Williams and "Ma T" after reaching greater heights as a gospel, jazz, and blues singer. Her legacy lives on in North Carolina, her home after leaving Memphis.

A Pictorial History

A.C. Williams (top row: left to right) and Cathryn Rivers Johnson (bottom row: third from left) left an indelible mark on many of The Teen Town Singers, including these youngers in this snapshot for posterity.

Bert Ferguson (left), WDIA's co-owner, chats with J. E. Walker, founder of Universal Life Insurance Co. and sponsor of The Teen Town Singers, and A. C. "Moohah" Williams in 1952, three years after Williams founded the chorale group.

TOP Photo: A crowning achievement for this group of youngsters at a WDIA event, as A.C. Williams stands proudly with them.

BOTTOM Photo: A family affair with A. C. Williams, his wife, Attee Williams (left), and Joan E. Patterson, his daughter.

A Pictorial History

The Teen Town Singers continue to fellowship together in this 2023 snapshot. They are (standing, left to right): James Nolan, Mary J. Cooper, Bobbie Joyner-Worthy, Lillie Huey, Glenda Mitchell, Pat Jones, Mary Bohanon, and Markhum L. Stansbury Sr. Seated (left to right): Dr. Ada Shotwell, Gwen Quirley, Imojene Stansbury (wife of Markhum L. Stansbury Sr.), and Barbara Griffin-Winfield.

In this 2019 snapshot, Glenda Mitchell (standing left to right), Fred Davis, and Joan Patterson, daughter of A. C. Williams, reflect on the era when they were Teen Town Singers. Seated, from left: Juanita Mitchum, Georgia Bland Gleese, and Pat Jones.

18

'I'm Telling You He Was Great'

Singing was **Percy Wiggins**'s first love. He and his brother, Spencer Wiggins, would listen attentively to The Teen Town Singers on Saturday mornings over the airwaves at WDIA-AM 1070 and eagerly wanted to join the group.

Percy Wiggins

"We just loved to sing," Wiggins said.

And just by happenstance, an opportunity came when he least expected it. It was Marvell Thomas and his sister Carla Thomas, Wiggins recalled, who talked to him and his brother Spencer about The Teen Town Singers.

The Thomases — the musically gifted children of the legendary Rufus Thomas, a WDIA luminary and soon-to-be an integral part of Stax Records' early success — were already onboard with the group.

"That's how we actually joined The Teen Town Singers," Wiggins explained, and added that A.C.

Williams, the group's founder and director, had come by the house to speak with their parents about them participating in the teen program.

"Everything was a go," said Wiggins. "They didn't mind us joining The Teen Town Singers at all, especially since A.C. was over the group — he and Cathryn Rivers Johnson.

"They knew A.C. Williams was a great guy and that he was a lover of teenagers and young people. They knew he wanted to help teenagers and make sure that they got on the right track."

Williams had gained his parents' trust and started coming over Saturday mornings to take Wiggins and his brother to WDIA for The Teen Town Singers' 10 a.m. show.

"We caught the bus back," he said.

Spencer Wiggins died February 13, 2023, at the age of 81. When the brothers were young upstarts, they lived at 805 Porter Street in the South Memphis community. Before Spencer's death, he had found success as a soul and gospel singer.

Of the seven Wiggins children (five boys and two girls), four were singers, including the two girls. Their parents, Spencer Wiggins Sr. and Lessie Lee Wiggins, had encouraged them to get involved in music.

"We were all one big happy family," Percy Wiggins said.

Wiggins was in the seventh grade at Porter Junior High School when he became a member of The Teen Town

Singers. He remained with the group after he matriculated at Booker T. Washington High School.

After school was dismissed on Wednesdays, The Teen Town Singers would rehearse at the YMCA at Linden Avenue and South Lauderdale. Wiggins was used to rehearsing songs. He sang in the choir at New Friendship Missionary Baptist Church at 724 East Georgia Avenue. So, rehearsing with his choral mates at the YMCA was a cinch.

"The practice sessions were great," he said. "We practiced until we got situations right. He [Williams] and Cathryn Johnson gave us our parts and things. We learned different songs."

There were songs Wiggins remembered singing "that I had never heard of before, that I never would have known about if it had not been for A.C. and Cathryn Johnson. So, I enjoyed the rehearsals."

Wiggins took the lead on some of the songs, singing first and second tenor. He also assisted Williams as the group's student director. The position wasn't a heavy lift for Wiggins but provided him with some responsibility and helped to develop within him a work ethic.

Wiggins said it was also an honor and an opportunity for him to lead and to ply his burgeoning skills as an up-and-comer in music whom Williams apparently trusted with the reins.

"I actually learned the songs and assigned various parts out" [to his choral mates], he said. "Sometimes I would do an arrangement on a particular song that I would bring to the table."

Wiggins said The Teen Town Singers had to be at the radio station at least 15-to-20 minutes before going on the air at 10 o'clock. "If we were late coming, A.C. would turn us around; he wouldn't let us in," he said. "That really gave us an opportunity to start being on time and being prompt."

It was a tough lesson that Wiggins and his choral mates would not forget — ever. "That really went a long way with us," he said.

Singing over the airwaves at WDIA and at other venues gave Wiggins a sense that he could expand his horizon someday as a professional recording artist when the opportunity was right.

Being a member of The Teen Town Singers was a kind of testing ground for the teenagers — particularly the ones like Wiggins who envisioned a career for themselves in music and entertainment.

Williams, however, provided the platform for The Teen Town Singers to showcase their talents before a live audience in addition to them singing over the airwaves at WDIA.

"We performed at the Starlite Revue and the Goodwill Revue," Wiggins noted. "We did background vocals behind some of the artists that they had at the Starlite Revue and the Goodwill Revue. It was an annual thing."

The Starlite Revue was held outdoors at Martin

Stadium, then home of the Memphis Red Sox, a Negro League baseball team, and one of a few venues where African Americans could gather.

Wiggins said he — along with Markhum Stansbury Sr., and his brother, Spencer Wiggins — were hired by Bert Ferguson, who co-founded WDIA, to set up folding chairs on the grounds of Martin Stadium for the people who came to view the show.

"There were a lot of chairs," he said, and added: "A.C. Williams was instrumental in getting us those jobs during that time."

The Goodwill Revue was held at the Ellis Auditorium in downtown Memphis. At both revues, Wiggins said The Teen Town Singers provided background vocals for the R&B balladeer Brook Benton, blues singer Theodore "Ted" Taylor, and other noted artists.

"We did some songs by Sam Cooke, too, but we didn't do any background vocals behind him," he said.

The Teen Town Singers sang background for gospel artists as well, said Wiggins, such as The Simms Twins (Bobbie and Kenny Simms), The Boyer Brothers, the Reverend Oris Mays, the Reverend Cleophus Robinson, The Raymond Raspberry Singers, The Davis Sisters, the Reverend James Cleveland, The Caravans, and others.

The teenagers were hitting all the right notes. Their voices were reverberating throughout Memphis and the Mid-South and their reputation soared. In addition to singing with The Teen Town Singers, Wiggins formed his own group within the choral group.

They called themselves the Five T's. The members were Wiggins, of course, his brother Spencer Wiggins, Marvell Thomas, Tyrone Smith, and John Ray Bunton.

"Whenever The Teen Town Singers would go out and perform, we would perform as well," he said. "We were the Five T's. We were all a part of The Teen Town Singers."

At BTW, Wiggins formed a gospel group with his brother Spencer and sister Maxine. They called themselves the New Rival Gospel Singers. "We had a 15-minute spot on WDIA on a Wednesday night," he recalled.

Wiggins spent six years with The Teen Town Singers. After graduating from BTW in 1961, he was awarded a $500 scholarship from WDIA and The Teen Town Singers to attend college. He chose Tennessee State University in Nashville, Tennessee.

"That $500 went a long way," said Wiggins, who used the money to purchase books and a few other items. "Back then it wasn't as expensive as it is today."

He was also singing R&B in a group with his brother Spencer Wiggins and songwriter/producer David Porter called The Four Stars. Porter, who also graduated from BTW in 1961, would go on to achieve fame as a house composer for Stax Records.

Wiggins's love for singing would graduate to another level while he was at TSU studying for his Bachelor of Arts and Science degree.

"I was a house vocalist for nightclubs in Nashville

called The New Era Club on Charlotte Avenue and Club Stealaway on Jefferson Avenue," he said. "Then I got an opportunity to meet a young man that became my manager."

Jerry Crutchfield, who lived in Nashville, began booking shows for Wiggins while he was still a student at TSU and juggling his schedule to accommodate his off-campus music career.

"I got an opportunity to be on some shows with a lot of big named artists in the business," he said, "like Curtis Mayfield and The Impressions, Jackie Wilson, The Whispers, The Five Stairsteps, and Junior Walker and the All Stars."

Wiggins also played the Howard Theater in Washington, D.C. "I was doing R&B during that time," he said, pointing out that Crutchfield had gotten him a contract with RCA Victor in 1966, ATCO Records in 1967, and Abet Records in 1968.

"The Work of a Woman," Wiggins's debut single, was released with RCA Victor. He recorded other singles with ATCO Records, an imprint of Atlantic Records, and Abet Records as well.

After completing his studies at TSU, Wiggins returned to his alma mater, BTW, where he taught remedial English and vocational mathematics to students in vocational classes at the school. He also taught night school, which included Speech 1 and 2 — all at BTW.

Wiggins taught school for four years. During that time,

"A.C. and The Teen Town Singers started rehearsing at Booker Washington High School in Cathryn Johnson's homeroom."

Because he had been a Teen Town Singer — and still considers himself one — Wiggins said he would stop by after school to help Williams with some arrangements on various songs.

After his stint at BTW, Wiggins sold insurance. "While I was in the insurance business, I was doing the music thing on the side," he said. "I stayed in the insurance business for 36 years. I retired in the insurance business."

He started with the National Life and Accident Insurance Company. That company was bought out by American General. "Then we were bought out by AIG (American International Group)," he said.

Wiggins said being a member of Williams's Teen Town Singers was the key that helped him to hone his gifts and increase his potential to become a successful soul singer and gospel artist.

He credits Williams for steering him in the right direction and preparing him at such a young age to be accountable for his actions, to always be on time, and to give his best.

He described his experience in the teen program as a springboard that launched him into the recording business and singing on stage in front of crowds as large as 15,000 to 30,000 people.

As for Williams, Wiggins said, "He loved us as a father

figure. Some of the people that were in the group came from broken homes. He took them under his wings as a father. He was just that type of person. He really helped us out a whole lot. I mean he was just terrific as a father."

He continued: "Some of the young people that had gone astray, he got them back on the right path. He made sure that a lot of them got scholarships to go to college when their parents didn't have the funds. A.C. stepped in and helped them out. He found the funds for those individuals."

Wiggins described The Teen Town Singers as a great outlet for teenagers. "It gave us a place to go and to be involved," he said. "It was a great experience for us. It really helped. He also taught us discipline and how to be on time for things."

He called Williams a great humanitarian.

"There's only one A.C.," he said. "When he was born, they threw the mold away. He was a great guy. I'm telling you he was great. He was a fantastic individual. He helped so many teenagers. He was responsible for a lot of people that are educators today."

Williams's love for his Teen Town Singers and his students in general extended beyond the classroom. While he had a penchant for being a tough disciplinarian, he was also known for being genuinely concerned about their well-being.

One day Wiggins was able to see clearly through Williams's tough façade. He recalled Williams coming to see him at the hospital bearing a financial gift and he could feel his heart.

Wiggins had had a serious operation. "I had a tumor on my liver," he explained. "They took my liver out, froze it for an hour and a half, cut the tumor out, and placed my liver back. I lost 40 percent of my liver."

Wiggins said Williams was sick himself but insisted on paying him a visit. "I had to come see about my son," said Williams, according to Wiggins. "He was just that type of person."

Wiggins has been married to Mary Wiggins for more than 50 years. They have a daughter, LaShunda Wiggins-Smith, and a granddaughter, Makiya Wiggins.

"Both of them sing — my daughter and my granddaughter," he said proudly. "But my wife does not."

Like her father, Wiggins-Smith graduated from TSU. Makiya, on the other hand, graduated from Alabama A&M University, a public, historically Black, land-grant university, in Huntsville, Alabama.

At 81, Wiggins doesn't sing much.

Over the course of his career, he said, "I thank the good Lord for the things that I was involved in during my lifetime. I attribute a lot of that to A.C. Williams."

19

'You Learned So Much'

Dr. Ada C. Shotwell sang alto, but she would do whatever was needed and be amenable to wherever A.C. Williams would place her to bring out the best in her as a Teen Town Singer.

Dr. Ada C. Shotwell

"I would do mostly whatever was needed," she said. "Basically, I would sing all of them [soprano, contralto, alto, tenor]. But I was an alto."

A graduate of Booker T. Washington High School, Shotwell spent two years with The Teen Town Singers, starting in grade eleven and fulfilling her commitment before graduation.

Membership in the teen program was a decision that Shotwell made without prior approval from her parents, the Reverend C.M. Lee and Amanda Lee. They accepted her decision nonetheless, she said.

"I told them what I was doing and they started listening every Saturday [on WDIA]. They sort of knew what was going on. It was no problem," said Shotwell, the youngest of the Lee's three children living on Majuba Avenue in South Memphis.

Two of Shotwell's best friends living in the same neighborhood had joined the group. "We lived so close together," she said. "On the days that they would have rehearsal, I really didn't have anyone to go with. So I had to get on the bus. I loved it after I got there.

"After I got in there, two weeks or so, I became one of them," she said, feeling like she was indeed a bona fide member of Williams's young cast of songsters and songstresses.

The adventure was exciting for Shotwell and she drew nigh to Williams, who utilized his skills as an educator to teach them how to carry a note, how to sound it off, how to enunciate, and how to manipulate one's voice and tone.

In addition to the above reference for good singing, Shotwell understood that Williams was trying to teach them the basic tools that a singer would need in their tool chest, such as rhythm, diction, breathing, pitch, and voice.

He was essentially their voice teacher.

"I had a lot of respect for him for what he did for us," she said. "He was just a good man. He just didn't take any junk. If you come in late, you were in trouble. It was respect...that we learned. Because there was no way in the world that I would be late. I was afraid."

Williams expected his choral group to remain discipline, said Shotwell, and added: "There was no cutting up with your friends in the neighborhood or anywhere else. [However], I enjoyed it — even when he got after me for wrongdoing."

He was a father to some of them, she said.

Shotwell knew she could sing. But the Teen Towners whose singing voices paled in comparison to the good singers, she said unequivocally, "I didn't think anyone should be up there if they can't [sic] sing. You don't have to do solos, but I feel you must know how to sing. You had to have the ability to sing. When he's teaching [during rehearsals] and you sing on Saturdays, you had to be able to sing, because there was no paper."

While singing may not have been the forte of every Teen Town Singer, Shotwell said the experience was fun and something that each member had to respect.

"We knew that people depended on us. We learned that when there is something you say you will do, you need to do it...if it is good. I think if you ask any of us, we will tell you that those were some of the best years of our lives.

"It really was a good lesson for any child to be in," she said. "You learned so much. So much."

Shotwell said being a member of The Teen Town Singers was a major part of her life. After graduating from BTW, she opted to attend Arkansas State University and chose education as a major.

"I taught for about three years," said Shotwell, teaching high school English in Tacoma, Washington, in 1967. In

1973, she took a job with the former State Technical Institute at Memphis, currently Southwest Tennessee Community College in Memphis (STCC). She would later become State Tech's Director of Academic Development.

Shotwell has a bachelor's degree from Southern University in Baton Rouge, Louisiana., her teaching certificate in English and Social Science from the University of California at Berkeley, a master's degree in guidance and personnel services from the University of Memphis, and a Ph.D. in higher education from the University of Mississippi.

She's also the recipient of several awards and honors, including Who's Who Among Black Americans and Who's Who Among America's Teachers. She's a life member with both the American Technical Education Association and the Association for Career and Technical Education.

In 2001, Shotwell, also the Dean of Liberal Arts and Education at STCC, received the Charles O. Whitehead outstanding service award, which recognizes educators who make significant contributions to technical education and the technical education division of the Association for Career and Technical Education.

Whitehead was president of the former State Technical Institute of Memphis.

Summing up her stellar career, Shotwell said, "I think I had a good life."

20

'It's A Family Affair'

I loved him [like a child would love her father]," **Barbara Griffin Winfield** said about A.C. Williams Jr. "We became very close. He was like that other father to me."

Barbara Griffin
Winfield

Winfield still hangs onto her precious memories of being a Teen Town Singer and sings with the group (even in her twilight years) at funerals for the Teen Towners who've transitioned from this life.

"There aren't many of us left, but we still stick together. It's a family affair," she said.

The affair is ongoing — even after the death of their founder and progenitor, A.C. Williams, who'd birthed the choral group and cultivated and promoted them for twenty-one years.

In retrospect, Winfield began singing as a little girl in the household with her parents, Arcola and Wilson O.

Griffin, two sisters and a brother in South Memphis.

"I used to listen to them [The Teen Town Singers] on the radio, and I'd sing along with them," said Winfield. "I was always singing from a little girl and I'd play the piano on the wall in my bedroom. So, I would sing and play. I was singing and playing ever since I was small."

She added with emphasis: "I cannot play the piano, sir."

Winfield's journey with The Teen Town Singers began when she was an eighth-grade student at St. Augustine Catholic School in the South Memphis community.

"I was in the eighth grade," she said, "and the strange part was he [Williams] was supposed to be searching for young people in nineth grade mostly, but I managed to get in there in the eighth grade."

Winfield then enrolled at Booker T. Washington High School, where other Teen Towners had matriculated. She graduated in 1958, but not before clocking in four years with the teen group.

Singing was Winfield's forte. In fact, she was one of Williams's pop soloists. "I was the pop singer...the pop soloist for the group when I was there," she pointed out. "That meant I had a solo practically every Saturday."

The fans, Winfield said, would swirl and express their delight in a frenetic way when she was on the microphone. "I loved it," she added. "And I even had a fan club in Corinth, Mississippi."

Winfield was also crowned "Miss Jubilect" and

represented WDIA and The Teen Town Singers. "I led the parade for the Cotton Makers Jubilee down Beale Street," she recalled. "My float led the parade. It was like being the Queen."

She was 16 and a junior at B.T.W. when she was chosen "Miss Jubilect" at the Beale Auditorium and crowned at The Historic Ellis Auditorium, a 10,000-seat, multipurpose arena at the corner of Poplar Avenue and Front Street. She bested 10 other contestants for the crown. Her prize for being selected the first "Miss Jubilect" was an "all-cotton wardrobe."

Throughout her tenure in Williams's teen choral group, Winfield immersed herself in the program and had a good time as a standout Teen Towner whose vocals were noticed — thanks to the opportunities that were afforded her and the others by Williams and his team.

But rehearsals were mandatory. They were opportunities for the Teen Towners to learn the songs, perfect their craft, and follow Williams's directions.

"Even though he was supposed to have been tough, he was a teddy bear," Winfield said. "He loved young people. He loved working with young people. He was very kind natured. He just smiled all the time. But when he was serious, you knew he was serious. And you didn't push him."

Williams would later describe Winfield as "hardworking, friendly, talented and sweet." She started with the group in 1953 and left in 1957.

When Winfield made her decision to go to college, she chose Arkansas State University. "I was in the choir, so I received a choir scholarship for music and sang for four years," she said. "All expenses were paid except for books. Guess who bought the books? A.C. Williams and The Teen Town Singers."

She continued: "I received scholarship money from the university, but the Teen Towners paid for my books. They didn't have the money to continue. My family didn't have money for college either. It was a big help."

The glory days are now a footnote in history for Winfield and her fellow Teen Towners. However, the bond that was established between Williams and his choral group of songsters and songstresses is still solid, unbreakable.

"We still get together at least twice a year. I think in the summer and before Christmas," Winfield said. "You know, we would have a little get together and we would sing as many songs as we can remember. We just have fun."

Fun is the operative word for Winfield and her experience as a Teen Town Singer. But then she added: "I just loved it!" She followed that point with a poignant phrase or what could be the motto for the surviving Teen Town Singers.

"Once a Teen Towner, always a Teen Towner."

21

'He Loved Us'

Booker T. Washington High School was **Mary J. Cooper**'s stumping ground from which legends in music and entertainment were nurtured and blossomed. The school also produced a handful of talented Teen Town Singers.

Mary J. Cooper

Cooper hailed from South Memphis with her three sisters. She had two half-brothers, she said, but they were much older. Her first foray into singing began when she was a little girl. Then she heard The Teen Town Singers on the radio.

Inspiration to join the group tugged at Cooper, who knew she could sing. "All of my life," she maintained. The music motivated her, the comradery impressed her, and increased her desire to be a part of something special and fulfilling.

After receiving the green light from her mother, she joined the eclectic body of teenagers on the precipice of becoming celebrities — all under the direction and guidance of A.C. Williams, founder of the teen group, and under the auspices of WDIA.

Her father, Washington Cooper, died when she was eight years old and her mother, Mary Cooper, who'd given her daughter her name, never married again. This left a void in Cooper's life within a fatherless household.

"He [Williams] was like my surrogate dad," Cooper said. "I loved that man...I'm telling you. He was like our father. He treated us all the same. He wasn't that easy, either.

"He didn't take no stuff. He didn't spoil us; he loved us," she said. "You know how you raise a child...you tell him that you love him. But you tell him when they're wrong and all that stuff."

But then Cooper developed a special relationship with Williams and enjoyed the comradery between her fellow Teen Towners for four years while she sang with them in the program.

"I didn't lead much, but I enjoyed The Teen Town Singers," Cooper said. "We were a closely-knit family. We will always be. Daddy taught us that. That's why we try to remain together.

"Of course, we were one of the first ones. The older ones...I know a few of them who are still alive," she said. "They would be in their nineties. That's a long time. So, we had all age groups. But mainly what we had in common was A.C. 'Moohah' Williams."

After Cooper's stint with the group, she moved out of town to attend a college in Indianapolis. She eventually went to work for South Central Bell, now AT&T. She retired as a manager.

Williams was very influential and impacted the lives of his young charges. Being a Teen Towner paid dividends in different ways, in some cases, for many of them.

During the latter part of Williams's life, Cooper worked with her surrogate father on a scrapbook with pictures. "I was at his resident when they [Williams and his wife, Attee] lived on Union Avenue [in the high-rise]," she said. "I would come there just about every week working on that book."

The scrapbook captured the history and essence of The Teen Town Singers with news clippings and photos, tracked the success of the members, highlighted Williams and his role at WDIA, and provided a window into Williams's thinking when he formed the teen group in 1949.

"I was so happy with that book," Cooper said. "I was out of town when he passed away. I don't know what they did with the book. I assumed they gave it to Joan [Patterson]," Williams's daughter.

Cooper had known Williams for a long time. She regrets not being in Memphis when he passed. Nevertheless, her affinity for him has never waned. He'd taken her under his wings — as a father would, she said. The others, too. He was 'daddy' to them as well.

"Yes, he was," she conceded. "Don't make me cry. That's all I could think about because I didn't have one."

Family members of Cooper's are buried in New Park Cemetery on Horn Lake Road in Memphis. Williams is buried there, too, along with his wife, Attee. Their final resting place is near the graves of Cooper's mother and sister.

"Whenever I go to change my mother's and my sister's flowers, I go over there to visit his and Mrs. Williams," she said. "When I go there and don't see any flowers, I get upset. I go and change the flowers because we are a family."

22

"He Was A Gentle Giant'

It was the consensus among The Teen Town Singers that A.C. Williams Jr. was dedicated, driven, laser-focused, sincere, and tough on his young charges — including those who'd just started with the choral group and those who'd graduated out of the program.

James Nolan

But according to **James Nolan**, Williams was "a gentle giant" and more than that. "He was my second dad," said Nolan, a welcome member of the group.

It was the comradery, the fellowship, and the rehearsals that Nolan enjoyed so much. "I wasn't a good singer," he said unabashedly, "but I loved to be there at the rehearsals and on radio on Saturday mornings.

"Although I wasn't a great singer, I was a Teen Towner. That alone made me great," he said, then added: "Mr. Williams didn't necessarily want talent, he wanted commitment."

James Nolan

Nolan was committed.

It all began at Booker T. Washington High School. "I was in the glee club," said Nolan, who was in the eleventh grade. "Cathryn Rivers Johnson was over the glee club."

Johnson was also the pianist for The Teen Town Singers. "That's how I got to be a part of the Teen Towners," he said. "It is something about being connected to that group that really set people apart."

According to Nolan, "Anybody could be a Teen Towner." But there was a catch, which was: "You started out as one, but that doesn't mean you'll stay there. You got to be obedient to Mr. Williams and do the right thing."

After graduating from BTW in 1958, Nolan said Williams asked him if he wanted a scholarship to attend college. "I told him no. I was tired of going to school," he said. "I wasn't an honor student. I chose to study what I wanted to study."

Nolan's favorite subject was chemistry. "I could look at a chemical equation and balance the equation just by looking at it. I was committed to that particular subject," he said.

He thought about attending Massachusetts Institute of Technology, better known as MIT, which is noted for its scientific and technological training and research.

"I really didn't know where MIT was. I didn't know what MIT meant," he said. "I wanted to go to MIT for this reason: Some of the books that I was studying from, that I would get from the library, were written by professors at

MIT."

He figured MIT was a good school. But he didn't pursue it. Instead, he decided he'd join the U.S. Air Force to help his father. "I had to do something to help him," he said.

Before Nolan could earn his wings in the Air Force, he had to take the Armed Services Vocational Aptitude Battery (ASVAB) test and be proficient in arithmetic reasoning, work knowledge, paragraph comprehension and mathematics knowledge.

"In electronics I made a 95. So that's what I ended up working in — electronics in the Air Force," said Nolan, whose job was working on radar equipment, air traffic detection radar, and then missile detection radar.

"The many jobs that I had wasn't common for a colored person to be working there. I'm still using the word 'colored' because that's what we were back then."

Nolan went on to work for the Xerox corporation. During those days, he recalled, white people challenged his intellect, his skill set, as if he were incapable of having a good job or performing assigned tasks with excellence.

"For a Black person to do the job that was done by a white person, you have to be twice as good," he said. "That's the way it's been all through my life. We were treated by white folks as second-class citizens."

In those days, Nolan took the best route that he knew to earn a decent and respectable living after his two-year stint as a Teen Town Singer had ended. He never regretted his decision.

"I am a product of the people in my past...and Mr. Williams was one of them," he said. "We are better people because of Mr. Williams and the Teen Towners."

Nolan didn't go into the music business or the entertainment business like some of the Teen Towners had done, "but whatever we went into, we are better because of what he [Williams] did for us."

He ended on this note: "He was a great man. He would do anything for us kids."

23

'It's A Bond That Will Never Die'

The Teen Town Singers knew what to expect if they didn't take A.C. Williams's non-negotiable rules of being on time seriously — no matter the circumstances.

Case in point: After **Bobbie "B.J." Joyner-Worthy** and her friends — fellow Teen Towners Barbara Johnson, Marilyn Jackson and Tina Bryant — arrived late for a Wednesday rehearsal, Williams enforced the rule.

"Mr. Williams shut the door," Joyner-Worthy remembered. "We were like three, maybe five, minutes late and we couldn't get in; we couldn't practice. So, if you didn't practice, you didn't sing that Saturday."

Bobbie "B.J." Joyner-Worthy

Arriving on time was a prerequisite for being in good standing as a Teen Town Singer. It was a lesson learned for Joyner-Worthy and her friends, and one that she'd never forgotten.

Bobby "B.J." Joyner-Worthy

"You just couldn't be late," she said. Her memory of Williams shutting the door still comes across her mind with resounding clarity. Sometimes "we would half walk and half run to get to practice, because you couldn't be late."

Joyner-Worthy got her start as a Teen Town Singer in tenth grade at Booker T. Washington High School when she was a member of Cathryn River Johnson's St. Cecilia Glee Club.

The year was 1962. Musically gifted since she was twelve years old, Joyner-Worthy was playing the piano at Mt. Zion Baptist Church at Main and Parkway and singing in the choir. She sang first alto.

"By the time I got to Booker T. Washington, I was still playing for the church when I joined the glee club," said Joyner-Worthy, adding that Johnson, the pianist for The Teen Town Singers, was her music teacher who would have her to play the piano sometimes.

"She also encouraged me to join The Teen Town Singers," said Joyner-Worthy, who joined the teen group with Tina Bryant, Barbara Johnson, and Marilyn Jackson.

"We had grown up together and gone all the way through elementary school together," she said. "We just liked singing. And all of us sang in our different churches. Marilyn and I went to Mt. Zion Baptist Church. Barbara went to Morning View Baptist Church."

They formed a singing group too. "We didn't have a name," she said. "We just got together and we would just sing together a lot. We just had a love for music. We thought we were extra special. It started from there."

Joyner-Worthy lived in South Memphis with her five brothers and two sisters at 1672 Latham Street. Her parents, Claude and Sallie Joyner, held the family together.

"It was a big fun family," she said. "I was the only person who had that undying love for music, even though my younger siblings sang in the choir at church."

Her mother demanded that "we all be in church and participate in church," she said. "You didn't go to church you couldn't do anything else but go to school. You couldn't have any other activities. We had to go."

The Joyner children had to be on time, too," she said. "We couldn't be late for church and Sunday school. When I played for the choir, the minister said, 'Look, [at] 10:45, hit the keys. I don't care if it's one person in the pews.'"

Since going to church was a prerequisite for Claude and Sallie Joyner's children to participate in any outside activity, Joyner-Worthy, who heeded their rules, was given permission to join The Teen Town Singers.

At BTW, it wasn't a stretch for her to take the bus home. She would hop on the 13 Lauderdale Waldorf and deboard at Latham and Waldorf and walk two blocks to get to her house.

On Wednesdays, "my dad would pick us up sometimes when we would have to go to practice," she said, and added: "He would pick us up when he could and drop us off at the Y[MCA]."

Bobby "B.J." Joyner-Worthy

Joyner-Worthy practiced at the YMCA on Lauderdale and Linden Avenue with the teen group and sang on Saturdays at WDIA. They also sang at other venues, including churches, schools, and at the Goodwill Revue and the Starlite Revue.

"Every now and then we would get to sing either before the show started, or something like that," she recalled. "I don't know how Mr. Williams did that, but he always, you know, had us around music. There was no big 'I' and little 'U'.

"We all were treated equally, whether you were a Carla Thomas or, you know, one of the others..." she said. "Everybody enjoyed the same dignity and respect. Of course, we gave it to him. We were all a group. All for one, and one for all.

"One of the rules that he had that I always appreciated was that you may not have been the best singer, or you may not have been the lead singer, but everybody in the group had some opportunity to lead some song at some point."

If a Teen Towner didn't have the courage to lead a solo, "Mr. Williams would say, 'Get up. You have to try. You don't know what you can do until you try.' It gave us confidence. We always appreciated that about him..."

She said this was a characteristic that was very important in her life.

Joyner-Worthy loves music as much as Williams enjoyed teaching it and cultivating the skills of young, talented kids. "He was absolutely dedicated to children and education and talent," she said. "And for those who had the talent for it, he wanted to help to build, cultivate, and expose you as much as he could.

"He gave us the audience," she continued. "And some of them, as you know, have gone on to be national, not just local, but national, worldwide. It's something that we will never, ever forget.

"It's been etched in with pride in our memory and in our lives. I hate that we didn't have the ability or the chance to pass it on to our children, because it's so many other venues now."

Williams was a surrogate father to some of The Teen Town Singers who may not have had a father in the home. "Some didn't have fathers present. I noticed they would call him Daddy," Joyner-Worthy said.

"I came from a two-parent home. I had a mother and a father and we did family things. So, my dad was just as involved with the boys — my brothers — teaching them life skills. My mother, of course, had the girls."

Though Williams was a father figure so some of Joyner-Worthy's choral mates, she noted, "I had a daddy. So, I never referred to him in that kind of term." But then "he helped a lot of kids. Sometimes they wouldn't have bus fare home. [And] he got to know your parents."

Williams would talk to the parents, she said. "He would tell them, 'When they're in my charge, Cathryn and I will treat them just like one of our own, and we're gonna love them just like our own.' He was like your own parent away from home."

Joyner-Worthy graduated from BTW in 1964. "We received a Teen Town scholarship," she said. "When you became a senior and you were graduating, everybody got that scholarship."

Her scholarship was $100, she recalled. "In those days that was a lot of money. We were riding high on that. But then I got a scholarship and went to LeMoyne Owen College."

She dreamed of attending Spelman College in Atlanta, Georgia, but her mother did not want her to leave home, even though she had received a scholarship to attend Spelman.

"So, I just made up my mind. I'd just stay here and go to LeMoyne," she said, and graduated in 1968.

After college, Joyner-Worthy returned to BTW, her alma mater, to teach eleventh grade English. "I loved going back to my alma mater to teach," she said. "It was just a beautiful experience, really. Those were some of the best days of my life."

In 1970, she was sent to Sherwood Junior High and spent one-year at the school as a secondary English teacher. It broke her heart that she had to leave BTW. Then she was moved to Whitehaven High School. "That was a great experience too," she said.

Joyner-Worthy spent a total of ten years in the school system. "I started doing real estate on the side," she said, and became an appraiser. "I was the first Black agent out here in Germantown. I kind of opened this market for other Black agents."

She's been a realtor now for 45 years. "I became a life member of the multi $1,000,000 club in 1987. I've been pretty consistent. I still work almost seven days a week."

When Joyner-Worthy thinks about Williams's legacy and what he's done for kids — and how she benefited — she often revisits one of his stringent rules: being on time. "It's still with me now," she said. "That's the way I think it ought to be. Time is money."

If an event doesn't start on time, "I get irritated," she added.

Many years have gone by and Joyner-Worthy still holds Williams in high esteem. "We just loved being in his presence," she said, taking the liberty to speak for the group. "We were a tight group; and those of us who are still living, we still feel that way about each other."

Thanks to WDIA, Joyner-Worthy said the radio station provided the platform from which some of The Teen Town Singers would use to springboard to successful careers as singers and musicians.

For others like Joyner-Worthy, "It gave us some notoriety," and called Williams one of the forerunners and "one of the drum majors to help spread the talent of young Black kids."

At the age of 76, a proud Joyner-Worthy said, "I'm going to be a Teen Town Singer...a part of this group...until we all die. That's just the way we feel. We were proud."

She described it as a bond that will never die. "It's because Mr. Williams brought us together like that. He always told us to stick together, to look out for each other, and to keep loving each other. That's what we've done."

24

'He Was A Great Male Figure For Me'

Markhum "Mark" L. Stansbury Sr. once remarked that he couldn't carry a tune in a bucket. Apparently, that didn't matter to Cathryn Rivers Johnson, he said, who sensed that something special was budding in her sixteen-year-old pupil.

Markhum "Mark" L. Stansbury Sr.

Stansbury was a member of Johnson's coveted glee club at Booker T. Washington High School, where she taught and played the piano for the glee club and for A.C. Williams's Teen Town Singers, a choral group that he founded in 1949.

Stansbury said he was in the tenth grade and hanging out in the school auditorium between classes when Johnson tapped him and asked him to report to her classroom. She had piqued his curiosity and he wanted to know what she wanted from him.

What Johnson wanted took Stansbury by surprise. "She invited me to join The Teen Town Singers," he said, and conceded that he never had an inkling of joining such a group. But then he consented and never regretted his decision.

"On Wednesdays and Fridays, we met down at the old Abe Scharff branch of the YMCA on Lauderdale and Linden Avenue," Stansbury said. "That may have been when I met Mr. Williams."

Stansbury said he wasn't the only Teen Town Singer of the lot who couldn't carry a tune in a bucket. Although he couldn't sing, he was in good company: There was another.

"My best friend, the late attorney Samuel B. Perkins, and I were the only two Teen Towners at the time known to not be able to carry a tune in a bucket. But Mr. Williams did not deny either one of us. He let us stay in and make contributions."

It was about "doing and helping young people," Stansbury pointed out, which was the impetus that led Williams to create a platform for inner-city youngsters to express themselves through the genre of music when he founded The Teen Town Singers.

"He taught us songs," said Stansbury, even though he didn't know the lyrics to some of them. "[But] he taught me how to try to sing. I never tried to lead anything" until he was asked to lead a song.

Although Stansbury had admired Elvis Presley since the seventh grade, he got the chance of a lifetime to witness the up-and-coming rock 'n' roll superstar perform on a flatbed truck that was converted into a stage on the parking lot of the newly opened Lamar Airways Shopping Center in the historic Orange Mound community on September 9, 1954.

With Elvis in mind, he remembered the moment he stood boldly in front of his peers and tried his darndest to sing an Elvis number that he took the lead on at Williams's behest while several of his choral mates stood around. They were "touching me, letting me know when to [start] and when to stop."

Though Stansbury couldn't remember the name of the song that he tried in vain to sing, he has always been an Elvis fan. He fared better listening to the legend and playing his music rather than trying to belt out an Elvis tune.

Raised by his mother, Eliza Markham Stansbury, in the Foote Homes housing project and at 378 Hernando Street — just south of downtown Memphis between Vance Avenue and Calhoun Street — Stansbury didn't have a father or a male role model other than Williams, "who was a great male figure for me growing up."

He said his mother and grandmother, Mrs. Mary Markham, raised him and his sister, Claudine. "It was two of us," he said. "After my grandfather died, my grandmother moved in to take care of and to raise my sister and me, along with my mom."

His mother, he said, was very supportive — even when

he was twelve years old and delivering groceries for Thompson Sundry at Mississippi Boulevard and Calhoun Street (now G.E. Patterson Avenue).

"I used to ride my bicycle to deliver cigarettes and beer and ice cream…for the people in the community," he said, believing it was his responsibility as a man to help support his family. But he was only twelve.

Stansbury had never met his biological father, Willie Stansbury. But he's never had a problem talking about him, either. Williams, however, would step into the role — not as a replacement, but as a surrogate who served the same purpose as a doting father and disciplinarian.

"He taught not only me but other Teen Towners how to be men and gentlemen," said Stansbury, "and how to respect your elders and all. And the most important thing that I learned from Mr. Williams was…If you tell somebody you're gonna do something, do it regardless, even if it's inconvenient to you."

Stansbury gravitated to Williams like some of his choral mates whose households were devoid of a dominant male figure. Like Stansbury, they, too, approved of Williams as their surrogate father and his disciplinary methods, as if The Teen Town Singers were indeed his own children.

Two of Williams's pet peeves, Stansbury pointed out, were timing and doing what you say you will do. He said Williams could not be swayed one way or the other from his stance on both. But then —

"If I tell you I'm going to see you at twelve, then be available before twelve. If you're right on time, you're late," said Stansbury, recalling Williams's stern teachings. "But don't call and say at the last minute that you can't make it unless you're going to the hospital or something...or unless you have died."

Because of Williams's insistence on being punctual, Stansbury is a stickler for being on time today. And he doesn't promise to do something and not keep his word. Williams, in essence, has left an indelible mark of Stansbury and his choral mates who continue to esteem their progenitor.

On Saturday mornings, The Teen Town Singers were on the radio from 10:00 until 10:30. "We were supposed to be there at nine for rehearsals before we went on the air," said Stansbury. "If you got there after nine, he would tell you, 'Buddy, where have you been?'

"He didn't care where you had been," he continued. "He'd tell you to hit the door. Sometimes he may tell you to take a two-week vacation or take a month vacation. If you tell him, 'Mr. William, the bus was late.' He would say, 'No, the bus wasn't late. You were late.'"

The lessons that Stansbury learned from Williams as a Teen Towner were deeply engrained in his conscience. They would stay with him throughout his life and guide him in his professional endeavors.

"So, as a result of my learnings, I tried to never be late," he said. "A lot of people at meetings would always say,

'Well, Mr. Mark is always going to be on time.'"

Even at St. Andrew African Methodist Episcopal Church, where Stansbury is a lifelong member. He joined the church when he was five years old and served more than 50 years on the trustee board and the Stewardship and Finance Committee.

"I was always on time," he said, and fell short of a scheduled meeting only if extenuating circumstances precluded him from being on time. And that was extremely rare, he said. "Those were some things that Mr. A.C. Williams taught me."

The Teen Towners called him "Daddy Williams," said Stansbury, now 80 years old. "All of us." During their Teen Town reunions and get-togethers years later when Williams was alive, "so many people would come in and say, 'Hey, Daddy' or 'How're you doing, Daddy?'"

They were aging as well as Williams and honored him annually — even after Williams's death in 2004 — for giving them a new perspective on life and stepping in as their "Daddy" when it counted the most.

Stansbury has two sons of his own: Markhum Stansbury Jr., an actor living in Los Angeles, California, and Marlon B. Stansbury, a teacher with Memphis and Shelby County Schools. He instilled those same principles and values in his sons that Williams had instilled in him and his comrades in the teen program.

"I share that with my sons," said Stansbury, and added, "When I'm talking to young people, I try to encourage them. I try to be positive and tell them encouraging things and always tell them about the five 'Ps' — Prior Planning Prevents Poor Performances."

It may have been a stroke of good luck that Stansbury would meet Williams by way of Cathryn Rivers Johnson. But when he met one of his idols, Nat D. Williams, another WDIA luminary when he was in the sixth grade, the encounter could be described as fate.

Stansbury, of course, would call it a blessing, nothing more, after meeting Nat D. Williams and interviewing him at such a young age. "I always was touched and wanted to be like Nat D.," he said. "I wanted to be in radio and be a newspaper person."

He said A.C. Williams knew he was desirous of working in radio as a Teen Town Singer and reached out to David James, WDIA's program director at that time. "He [Williams] said [to James], 'You say you like this boy. Give the boy a job.'"

Stansbury was in the eleventh grade when an opportunity presented itself. Theo "Bless My Bones" Wade, then a popular gospel personality at WDIA, was out sick and had to have surgery, according to Stansbury. "The doctor said he could work, but he just couldn't drive. So, the station hired me to drive Brother Wade to the radio station every morning."

Stansbury now had his foot in the door at WDIA. While Wade was on the air spinning gospel tunes and hamming it up for the listening audience, "I would be standing in the studio watching this control board operator work and felt I could do it if I had an opportunity."

Once again, an opportunity arose. The control board operator took a week off from the radio station. While he was vacationing, Stansbury said James, the program director, filled in as the control board operator.

"That morning, Mr. James was talking to me and said, 'You think you can do this?' I said, 'I sure do.' He said, 'You better.'" Stansbury wanted to know why James would ask him if he could operate the control board. He got his answer.

"Because you gonna do it starting next week," said Stansbury, quoting James.

Stansbury was eighteen and a new hire at WDIA. "That's the way I was hired," he explained, and began running the control board. He also read the news over the air five minutes before the hour, which was customary.

Later, Stansbury would find a way to attend Lane College, a private historically Black college in Jackson, Tennessee, and continue to work at WDIA on the weekend.

Nat D. Williams and A.C. Williams had been his mentors at the radio station. But there was another mentor: Ernest C. Withers, the noted civil rights photojournalist, whom Stansbury met as a young budding photographer. He asked the distinguished photographer in a letter if Withers would take him under his wings as an apprentice.

Withers consented and Stansbury learned the rudiments of photography. In 1959, the radio station sent him to a journalism conference at Lincoln University in Jefferson City, Missouri.

"I always wanted to go to the University of Memphis (then-Memphis State University)," said Stansbury, speaking to a reporter in 2022 from *The Tennessee Tribune*, a Black weekly newspaper in Nashville, Tennessee. "But that was never to be."

Lincoln University was the alternative because of its journalism department. Stansbury had graduated from Booker T. Washington High School in 1960 but could no longer attend the university.

"I knew I was going to drop out and I always wanted to be in college," said Stansbury, who decided he'd contact the iconic photographer and one of his mentors.

"He taught me a lot. I learned how to process film in his darkroom," he said. "When he would go out of town, I would run the office for him. When he was in town, sometimes I would go and shoot pictures for him."

Over lunch one day, Stansbury said Withers thought of ways to get him back in school. He said Withers talked to Thaddeus Stokes, then-editor of the *Tri-State Defender*, a Black weekly newspaper in Memphis, as well as A.C. Williams and Nat D. Williams.

"Each one of them wrote a letter on my behalf [to the president of Lane College, the Reverend Dr. Chester Arthur Kirkendoll]," said Stansbury, who would go on to matriculate at the historically Black college in Jackson, Tennessee.

Markhum "Mark" L. Stansbury Sr.

While attending Lane College, Stansbury served as a photojournalist for the *Tri-State Defender, Jet* Magazine, and *Ebony* Magazine. He would go on to work as a news anchor, and he has been a popular gospel radio personality at WDIA for more than 60 years. Stansbury received his B.A. degree in history from Lane in 1966.

The relationships that Stansbury forged over the years have benefited him immensely. He served as assistant to four presidents of the University of Memphis. He also served as interim president of Shelby State Community College and vice president of advancement at LeMoyne-Owen College.

He also served as Shelby County Field Director for the Governor's Memphis Office and was tapped by then-Tennessee Governor Ned Ray McWherter to serve as his special assistant.

Stansbury's star has shone bright throughout his career endeavors. He was the first person of color to work in management at Holiday Inns, Inc. in the early days, for example, and worked as a reporter and copy editor for *The Commercial Appeal* newspaper. An award-winning photographer, he photographed six United States presidents and captured other historic images throughout history.

In addition to his work in higher education, photography, and as the weekend gospel announcer and host of "Sunday Afternoon's Best Gospel" at WDIA-AM 1070, Stansbury is a founding member of Diversity Memphis, a non-profit that promotes education, social justice, and peace in the Mid-south community.

He has also received numerous awards and served on various boards.

Stansbury attributes his career successes to A.C. Williams — along with Nat D. Williams and Ernest C. Withers — "who encouraged me, along with God, and made me who I am today." He refers to WDIA, the station's on-air personalities, and The Teen Town Singers as a big family.

"We were a lot of siblings," he said, noting there were more than 700 alums that Williams had touched in one way or another when they were Teen Town Singers not yet ready for the world. The survivors, however, have no problem telling anyone within earshot that Williams provided the platform for them to spread their wings.

Stansbury produced a letter from his archives that Williams had written to him in 1977 and sent it to his home to express his appreciation of Stansbury's thoughtfulness towards him and his complimentary letters of his work over the years.

The letter is dated April 11. Stansbury's birthday is April 5. It was a touching tribute to a Teen Towner that Williams had followed over the years and admired from a distance.

"It was great," said Stansbury, crediting Williams for molding him into the man that he is today. He treasures the letter and its author, A.C. "Moohah" Williams.

Markhum "Mark" L. Stansbury Sr.

Dear Mark:

For many years since you were in the 7th grade, at least you have written to me. Some were requests, some were points of information you thought I should have. But most were complimentary letters on my work and my life. You will never know how much your interest in me is meant. Some of your letters and the many other thoughtful things you have done came in when I was at a low point, when I needed a lift. Thank you for caring and loving your old daddy. Now I must decrease and you must increase. I want you to know that you did a matchless job of production on the NAACP Freedom Fund dinner. Others got much of the credit, but you deserve more than them all. You coordinated a myriad of complex personalities and preferences into a cohesive, enjoyable, and profitable night. I don't think anybody else could have done it as well. I also want you to know that I am extremely proud of the loyal, dedicated, hardworking, professional way that you have advanced your career at Holiday Inns. Continue to make no mistake, you are being noticed. Your work with Holiday Inns and your complete support of so many worthwhile community efforts are fast, making you one of Memphis's most valuable young citizens. As long as you combine your hard work with dedicated service to mankind and asking God's guidance first, there is only one way for you. That's up. I am proud I know you.

Love from Daddy,
A.C. Williams
WDIA Community Relations Director.

Stansbury said he visited Williams for the last time when he languished in the hospital. It wasn't long before he was gone. Stansbury blames himself, rather than WDIA, for not stepping up to the plate to properly honor Williams and his legacy.

"I just knew the station would probably be the one to do something for him," he said, "although I, along with Fred Davis, Mary Jeanne Cooper, Glenda Greer, and Joan Patterson, were there doing what we could to keep The Teen Town Singers alive."

He added, "Now, tell the Lord, thank you!"

25

'He Was The Only Daddy I Knew'

He was the only daddy I knew," said **Joy Harvey Plunkett**, giving deference to A.C. Williams, the love of her life. He was her father away from home, she said, who was there for her when she needed a father the most.

"He was the daddy I knew for about fifteen years," said Plunkett, recalling her relationship with Williams, her godfather, and his family. "I remember his wife, his daughter. We were all close."

Joy Harvey
Plunkett

Her grandmother, she pointed out, used to clean Williams's home at 861 South Lauderdale. That's how close the two families had become, and how she and Williams had bonded.

"But if there was a problem, we would go to that front room; that was the conference room," said Plunkett, also recalling how Williams helped with her reading and comprehension.

For example, Williams would deconstruct a paragraph, she explained, to help her understand the context and the meaning of the paragraph. "You tell me what you understand with that paragraph," she said, quoting Williams, whose penchant for teaching was evident and widely known.

Plunkett was a little girl then and one of many young kids whom Williams, the venerable founder and director of The Teen Town Singers, took under his wings earlier in her life, and taught and directed her as well after she joined the incomparable teen choral group.

Always in teaching mode, Williams's relationship with Plunkett differed to some degree from the hundreds of Teen Town Singers that he had taken under his wings. It was a special bond per se, much like a father and his daughter, and one that Plunkett would treasure for a lifetime.

Her stories about Williams are precious, unforgettable, and tugs at the heartstrings; stories of a surrogate father and a little girl who holds on and never let go for any reason — even after she had become an adult and now a senior.

Take this story, for example: "When Daddy would get through with his radio program [on WDIA], we would go up to Four Way Grill (a historically Black-owned restaurant at the corner of Mississippi Boulevard and Walker Avenue)," Plunkett recalled, "and sit at the bar and get those famous buttered biscuits and jam."

Saturdays were special, too, she said, when Williams

would spend quality time with her and watch some of her favorite kid shows on TV. "We would watch 'Sky King,' 'Casper the Friendly Ghost', and I would have my Oreo cookies and milk."

Williams was her protector, Plunkett explained, her guardian per se. "Nobody messed with me," she said matter-of-factly. "If I was sick, he was right there for me."

And she was always there for him and with him — even at church, where Plunkett worshiped with Williams at Salem Gilfield Missionary Baptist Church. "My play mom was Cathryn Rivers Johnson (the church pianist and pianist and co-director of The Teen Town Singers)," she pointed out.

When Williams was being honored in the early sixties (circa 1962) for his work at WDIA and his civic work in the community, Plunkett was there at the Abe Scharff YMCA with Williams and his family one Saturday night for a "This is Your Life" program.

For the sake of posterity, a newspaper photographer captured a tender moment of Williams on stage with his grandson Eric (seated on his lap), his daughter Joan E. Patterson (who was Mrs. Joan Strickland at that time and married to Frank Strickland of Chattanooga, Tennessee), Hattie Smith (a family friend), and Plunkett, (formerly Joy Harvey), who was a young teenager.

Plunkett grew up in South Memphis in a home at 89 South Parkway — not far from where the Williams family lived. She graduated from Carver High School in 1968.

"I was one of the teenagers...one of the first ones to sing

'Here Comes Peter Cottontail' (a popular Easter song composed in 1949 by Steve Nelson and Jack Rollins) as a little girl," Plunkett remembered when she sang with The Teen Town Singers. "Then I sang at the Goodwill Revue and the Starlite Revue."

Plunkett received a scholarship in music from a WDIA sponsor, Big Star, "when they had the little talent shows when I was at Carver High School and with The Teen Town Singers," she said.

After graduation, Plunkett matriculated at Arkansas Agricultural, Mechanical and Normal College (AM&N), which is now the University of Arkansas at Pine Bluff, a historically Black university. She graduated from the university with a Bachelor of Arts degree in biology.

"Well, I graduated with a BA in biology, but ended up in banking," said Plunkett. "I worked at Union Planters Nation Bank for 20-something years and took an early out. My husband thought I was gonna go work somewhere, but I started selling Mary Kay cosmetics."

The memories that Plunkett has stored in her memory bank of Williams — or "Daddy," whom she continues to cherish and esteem — have shown no signs of fading but remain as sharp as they were when Williams was still among us.

"He was my daddy!" she said unabashedly, absolutely.

Plunkett still has an affinity for music. "I teach piano lessons on Mondays and Tuesdays," she said. "They say I can sing, but I read music very well."

Summing up her experience as a Teen Town Singer, she said: "It was wonderful." And Williams? "I loved him."

26

'I Just Wanted To Be A Part Of Them'

When **Timothy McGuire** was a student at Manassas High School, he had an opportunity to join A.C. William's Teen Town Singers. He could sing tenor, he said, but he decided to join the school band and play the trombone, a brass instrument that he could extract from it a deep, melodious register.

Timothy McGuire

"I was in the ninth grade at Manassas, and I was in A.C.'s homeroom. I took a biology class from him, too," he said.

McGuire recalled the day he could hear the melodious voices of The Teen Town Singers reverberating across the campus. "I didn't go to the room where the Teen Towners were," he said. "I kept right on to the band room and got in the band."

He played trombone during the three years that he was a student at Manassas. After completing the eleventh grade, he packed up and moved to Detroit, Michigan, and stayed nearly a year in the "Motor City." His plan was to go to night school and work during the day. But that didn't work out, so he returned to Memphis.

"I came back and they had a night class at Booker T. Washington," McGuire remembered. "I came back and went to night class to get my diploma so I could work in the daytime."

He continued: "When I come back from Detroit, The Teen Town Singers were on the radio. I would listen to them all the time. I just wanted to be a part of them, because I was still a good friend of Mr. Williams's. He was a good inspiration to me."

After obtaining his diploma, McGuire began working with Williams. "But I was kind of in touch with him all alone," he said, "and hung out with him after high school. I helped him out back at Manassas."

McGuire had finished high school and met the requirements for graduation, or, in his case, a diploma. But Williams had allowed him to join the choral group anyway, even though The Teen Town Singers were junior and senior high school students whose membership in the group had generally ended after graduation.

"I was kind of an assistant to A.C. Williams," he explained. "And I sang right there with them."

When the Goodwill Revue and the Starlite Revue were underway and drawing a robust following, McGuire said he was at both entertainment "revues" to help Williams by collecting money from the sale of tickets at various locations in the city on Saturday mornings.

"I would make the ones [locations] when he [Williams] was on the air," he said. "When he got off, we would go to Clarksdale and Tunica (both in Mississippi), and other places, and pick up money from tickets that were sold."

McGuire noted that he also assisted Williams by rounding up kids to help sell souvenir booklets at both the Goodwill Revue and the Starlite Revue. "It was a great experience," he said.

Originally from Brunswick, Tennessee, an unincorporated community in Shelby County — approximately 21 miles from the City of Memphis — McGuire said his family moved to the city in 1944 when he was nine years old.

He grew up with his parents, Beatrice and Timothy McGuire Sr., and his two brothers and three sisters in a modest home on Lewis Street and Vollentine Avenue, a relatively short distance from Klondike, a community in North Memphis.

The McGuire home was walking distance from the church, Vollentine Baptist Church, where he once worshiped and where he directed the "young people's choir" and the male chorus.

He also spent several decades worshiping at Union Valley Baptist Church on East McLemore Avenue in South Memphis. "I directed the senior choir and the male chorus at Union Valley Baptist Church for a long time, too," he added.

He served on the church's deacon board as well.

McGuire was eager to join the workforce after high school, which was his goal when he left Memphis for Detroit in his senior year. An opportunity finally materialized when he landed a job in the shipping department at The Humko Corporation, a manufacturing plant that produced vegetable oil products.

"I left Humko in '57 and I started at Kellogg's in '58," he said, and added: "I stayed there until '95. I worked all over the plant [at Kellogg's]. I was in supervision for two and a half years. I was in the shipping department."

McGuire was the first Black man hired at Kellogg's and the second Black supervisor in the warehouse. Before his retirement, he'd become a part of the Maintenance Oiler and Mechanic Department.

Between high school and the workforce, McGuire took the hand of Allene Coleman in holy matrimony. Two children were born to this union: Rholedia and Kennard McGuire. Unfortunately, the couple parted ways in 1974, and he married Vivian McGuire in 1981.

While laboring at the Kellogg's plant, McGuire ventured into another realm of labor: entrepreneurship. "I was kind of planning on going into the nightclub business," he said with certainty.

Before McGuire could actualize his plan, he talked to Williams about it. "He told me, 'Tim, you don't need no nightclub. You're a Christian man. You're a family man. And being in a nightclub business, you don't need this. Your kids could be exposed to that.'"

McGuire surrendered that idea. "That's the reason I changed," he said. "I wanted something where I could take my kids. So, I opened a skating rink on Beale Street."

McGuire had always dreamed of owning his own business. As it turned out, he opened the roller-skating rink in 1970 inside the Historic Hippodrome building, where he once skated as a kid.

In fact, he was renting the building. But then he shut the doors in 1979 following an unsettled dispute with the landlord over high rent payments and infrequent repairs — or no repairs at all — to the building.

Believing that a roller-skating rink was a good and safe investment for the community, McGuire stepped up his game in 1973 and bought a lot at the corner of McLemore near Rainer with plans to open a second facility.

The Southside Skating Center was soon completed. It was fully equipped, too, bathed in soft light, and the era's disco music blared as skaters whirled around the rink with confidence and measured speed. McGuire was 47 years old then and, according to the *Tri-State Defender*, he was the only Black man to own a skating rink within a three-state area.

"I stayed there [at Southside Skating Center] from '79 to '85," he said. "All that time I was working at Kellogg's."

Rholedia McGuire worked with her father at the skating rink until she matriculated at The University of Tennessee, Knoxville. Kennard McGuire, then 15 and a student athlete at Hamilton High School, was an assistant manager.

Kennard McGuire would go on to play football as a wide receiver for both the University of Tennessee and the National Football League's New England Patriots until a knee injury forced him to end his football career. Now he represents some of the NFL's most notable players via MS World LLC, his own premiere sports agency.

Rholedia McGuire would go on to marry Stanley Morgan, who also played the position of wide receiver for the New England Patriots (13 seasons), and the Indianapolis Colts (one season). He retired in 1988.

Meanwhile, Rholedia was teaching Family and Consumer Science, Nutrition and Foods, Consumer Economics, and Textile and Apparel in the Shelby County Schools district. She taught more than twenty-one years and once owned her own business, Rholedia's Boutique, for more than 15 years.

McGuire acknowledged that he couldn't remember much these days, considering his advanced age. But what he hasn't forgotten was his relationship/friendship with A.C. Williams and his tenure with The Teen Town Singers.

"It was a good experience," he said, "because you learned a lot from being in The Teen Town Singers [program]. It was a good relationship to bring a young human together...a group of kids that was from high schools in the city."

McGuire said he was musically gifted in those days — to some extent, he added — and credits Williams for setting the example that he and his choral mates followed to become productive and successful adults.

"Yeah, of course!" he replied when asked if Williams's teachings had added value to his life. "Especially in music," he said. "You know, like learning how to direct a choir," which McGuire had spent years perfecting the art at both Vollentine Baptist Church and Union Valley Baptist Church.

"A.C. was such a good inspiration for me," said McGuire, who keeps in his memory bank those wonderful and vivid memories of himself and Williams, whom he thought very highly of in those days as "a wonderful man...and a good teacher. He still conjures up pleasant and consoling memories today when Williams crosses his mind.

Williams was laid to rest in 2004, but McGuire has no problem retrieving the memories they once shared. Others may have faded, but he seems to hold on to the ones that he cherishes the most.

In 1954, Williams helped create the WDIA Goodwill Fund, Inc., a non-profit organization that provided transportation to schools for disabled Black children, doled out college scholarships to high school seniors, funded Little League teams in the region, and established boys' clubs.

McGuire is proud of a plaque that hangs in his home that displays an engraved image of a little boy standing adjacent to a man. Over their heads, in a bold font, are the words *Founders Club*. The inscription below their feet says:

Goodwill Boys Club of Memphis, founded April 9, 1967. Giving Thousands of Boys the Opportunity to Achieve Greatness.

McGuire has served on the WDIA Goodwill Board of Directors for decades since the 1960s. He has been the treasurer and financial secretary for just as long. "Anything pertaining to finance," he said, explaining his duties, including writing checks.

Now that McGuire is approaching the age of 90, he's quite content, having raised successful children, served God and His people, and watched his entrepreneurial dreams come true, all while planning to live the rest of his life with his wife, Vivian, in their quaint little neighborhood.

On top of all that, McGuire has never forgotten A.C. Williams.

One of his favorite scriptures is found in Isaiah 40: 31, the King James Version: "But they that wait upon the Lord shall renew their strength; they shall mount up with wings as eagles; they shall run, and not be weary; and they shall walk, and not faint."

The scripture is a testament to McGuire's unwavering faith and his longevity.

27

Williams Wasn't Shy About Enforcing The Rules

Under A.C. Williams's tutelage, The Teen Town Singers learned more than just belting out melodious songs, performing before a live audience, and entertaining WDIA's listening audience. In fact, it was par for the course and expected of them to be responsible, punctual, courteous, make no excuses, and give it their best shot as a member of this coveted group of future superstars.

Even with Williams's stringent rules in place, the high schoolers sang gleefully, exceeded expectations, and left a lasting impression on the community, countless supporters, and the listeners in person and over the airwaves.

However, those memories of yesteryear continue to elicit positive comments and a warm and fuzzy feeling from the surviving members of the famed choral group whenever Williams's name is evoked. They're now in the twilight of their lives and still relish being called Teen Town Singers and members of the coveted "glee club" per se.

After Williams founded the group in 1949, the membership would grow exponentially each year. And each member would feel a part of something that was much bigger than themselves. They would go on to make a name for themselves in life with a head start that Williams had given them.

A few of them in this special group of talented youngsters from Memphis's inner-city schools — Manassas, Hamilton, Carver, Booker T. Washington, and other high schools — were impacted to some degree by their extenuating circumstances, such as not having a father in the home.

Despite their circumstances, Williams kept the door open to all who desired to join The Teen Town Singers. Many of them in the group referred to him as "Daddy," a term of endearment and recognition of Williams as a father figure and a symbol of authority and strength. For Joy Harvey Plunkett, he was that and more — a father that she had known for at least fifteen years of her life.

But after Williams took the bevy of teenagers under his wings and nurtured them — as a doting father would — he demanded accountability, respect, and hard work. He treated them as if they were indeed his own biological children and loved them unconditionally. He also admonished them, if needed, while steering them to a college or university after graduation, and, thereafter, to successful careers.

Enforcing The Rules

He also expected The Teen Town Singers to follow his directives, his pre-set rules, which were chiseled in stone, noted Joan E. Patterson, Williams's daughter, or they would be asked to leave the group — for Williams didn't tolerate foolishness and lollygagging during practice or anywhere else. He was serious and razor focused on the young men and women in his charge and wanted nothing better than to make them better versions of themselves.

"Daddy didn't play. He was a strict disciplinarian. He was the same with me as you," said Patterson, underscoring her point that Williams just demanded respect. "He was just one of those type people. He didn't have to say much [to get your attention]."

Patterson knew this to be a fact from first-hand experience. That's because she lived with the famed radio personality and choral director and remained under his tutelage as a Teen Town Singer for six years.

"If you were late getting to practice, you may not sing. If you didn't come to practice or rehearsals, you wouldn't sing on Saturday. So those were his strict rules," she said. "A lot of kids didn't have great voices, but as long as you were willing to accept the discipline, you were in."

The Teen Town Singers were apprised of the rules at the onset of joining the group and complied — at least most of them, said Patterson, who had better sense not to run afoul of her father's rules. She didn't want to be on the opposite end of his patience and tolerance. However, like any other teenager, she wanted to do her own thing.

Patterson was rather young when she started as a Teen

Town Singer. She started singing with the group when she was in sixth grade. "It was nepotism, because Daddy knew that I could sing," she explained. "He encouraged me to join, even though I was younger than most of them at that time. Usually, they waited until you got into high school. In those days, high school started at nineth grade."

A Teen Town Singer for six years, Patterson sang with the group throughout high school — which ended after she graduated from Booker T. Washington High School. During her tenure with the group, if her father's rules were broken, she would, more than likely, suffer the same fate as any other member of the choral group.

"He didn't play," Patterson reiterated.

Markhum L. Stansbury Sr. also dared not run afoul of Williams's rules. He would arrive at least thirty minutes early for rehearsals, for example, or to any venue where The Teen Town Singers were singing or making an appearance. Arriving on time was considered late, he said, and continues to employ this practice without fail.

He pointed out that Williams was known to shut the door and wouldn't allow a Teen Towner to enter if they arrived late for practice during the week and on Saturdays when the group performed on the radio at WDIA. Was Williams teaching his young charges the importance of showing up on time in every aspect of their lives?

Stansbury thinks so — for being tardy was a non-starter, he added. After arriving late one day to sing, Williams said, according to Stansbury, "Where do you think you're going, Little Bud? Take a vacation." He did — for two weeks.

Others would agree that Williams always meant business about his choral group following the rules — no lollygagging, no disruptions, no outbursts — including Carla Thomas, who felt the brunt of Williams's annoyance of her during a Wednesday evening rehearsal. What transpired that day between Williams, the serious-minded teacher, and Thomas, then a senior and an up-and-coming singer from Hamilton High School, was anything but cordial.

It was a disagreement pretty much that caused Thomas to fume. She began by pointing to the relationship between Williams and her father, Rufus Thomas, who enjoyed watching boxing with him on Monday nights at the Thomas household on Kerr Avenue in South Memphis.

"He and Dad used to sit there on boxing night. Mother [Lorene Thomas] would pop popcorn and we would all sit there watching boxing," said Thomas, reminiscing. "We loved for him to come over and they would make all kinds of noise."

At rehearsal that Wednesday evening, Thomas said Williams had given her a song to learn on a piece of paper. The Teen Towners were rehearsing at the YMCA at Lauderdale and Linden that day and they all had to learn their parts before going on air the upcoming Saturday at WDIA.

"Fannie Farmer was my friend from Carver," Thomas noted. "I didn't know too many people from Carver. She would make faces at me. She knew I was kind of shy. As long as he let me sit there and learn it [the song], I was fine."

Williams was busying himself with Cathryn Rivers Johnson who was at the piano, she said, and "pulled me up in front of everybody. Of course, I'm just learning the song and I'm going to make some mistakes."

In the process of learning the song, Thomas said Farmer was making faces, grimacing at her, and sticking out her tongue. "I'm sitting over there laughing. I'm doing it back at her," she said, chuckling.

"He was trying to tell Ms. Johnson something on the piano and turns around and sees me doing all this — I guess thinking I'm not serious. Mind you, I'm in there since I was eleven years old. He turns around, looked at her [Farmer], and said, 'Why are you doing that to her?' Then he snatched my paper and said to me: 'You need to go sit down.'

"I don't have to go nowhere," Thomas remembered telling Williams while her fellow choral mates were gawking in surprise. "Everybody was probably thinking, *'I've never seen them fall out. They get along so good.'*"

Williams had made Thomas his pop singer. The one before her had graduated, said Thomas. So, her role with the group was apparently important and one of the keys to the success of The Teen Town Singers since Thomas was deemed one of Williams's better singers.

Now seething because Williams had asked her to sit

down, Thomas responded rather hastily in front of the wide-eyed teenagers, including Cathryn Rivers Johnson, on that Wednesday evening, who, confusingly, didn't know what to make of Thomas's outburst. "I don't have to go anywhere but home," she told Williams. "And guess what? That's where I'm going."

After that eventful evening, Thomas didn't show up for Friday's rehearsal at the YMCA and on that Saturday morning when The Teen Town Singers were on the air at WDIA. And the song that Thomas was supposed to learn, after holding Williams responsible for snatching it from her, was absent from the repertoire of songs the teenagers would sing over the airwaves.

"Now boxing night comes back around," said Thomas, noting that Williams was at the house again on that Monday evening watching boxing with her father.

"Momma was going to cook popcorn and make some Kool-Aid," she said, "which she always did." Thomas wasn't fazed. She could care less about watching boxing at that time with her father and Williams, and said, "Let them have fun in there because I'm not going to be in there."

"Whoa!" her mother exclaimed, according to Thomas. "You used to love to sit there and watch them act crazy."

She said Williams had come over early this time to the Thomas household before boxing commenced. "He told my mother what happened. He said, 'Do you know she didn't come Friday or Saturday?'"

According to Thomas, her mother's response was, "Oh!

But she didn't tell me what really happened. She just said she wasn't going back."

Thomas said she heard them talking. "But I don't know until this day if he told her the truth. He did tell her that we'd fallen out and that he was concerned. I was there so long [in the group], he was surprised that I didn't come back. I doubt he'd have said that it was his fault, knowing A.C."

While the grown folks were conversing, Thomas said she was back in the den watching TV. "He came back and said, 'Heyyyy! You haven't been to rehearsal. What's going on?'" he asked her.

There was something indeed going on in Thomas's head. So, she said to him, "I got a lot of other things I got to do." She was adamant about not coming back to the group. But then Williams said to Thomas, "You need to come back. We're still working on that song."

Thomas remembered thinking about what she was going to do on Wednesdays and Fridays since she would no longer be a member of The Teen Town Singers. "When you're sixteen and seventeen," she reasoned, "you got some other things going."

She said Williams and her father would go on to watch the boxing contest. But she refused to watch it with them. When the next Wednesday rolled around, Thomas was back in the group.

"I didn't cry or anything," she said about her "fallout" with Williams. "I learned something about myself: I don't like injustice. I don't like mess. Nothing bothers me like that until something happens. Then I don't know when I'm going to react. I try to stay out of situations where I have to do some heavy confronting."

But then she pointed out that Williams was just being a teacher — a stern one at that.

"I guess it was his mood," she suspected. "He would put people out for a week or two — however he was feeling. He would suspend them. He did that to some of his best singers. Whenever he got into his 'teacher thing,' it's like, 'Okay, I'll suspend you' — like suspending you from school or expelling you."

Some of the teenagers that Williams had suspended didn't always come back, Thomas said, "which he thought they would. I was a senior and trying to learn a song. We had rehearsals every Wednesday and Friday. We had to learn it off the paper."

When looking back on the flare-up with Williams, Thomas said this with complete honesty: "I have no bad feelings. I didn't like it, but I didn't dislike him. But he knew I was always in his corner."

The Teen Town Singers today would agree that Williams was serious about the teen program and his intention to steer his young charges in the right direction. Even though he was laser focused and "strict," they believed he wanted the best for them.

In short, Thomas's self-dismissal and her return to the fold no doubt benefited the choral group and helped to catapult her to heights that she had not gone before skyrocketing as a singer.

28

Promoting The Teen Town Singers and WDIA

The Teen Town Bulletin — the brainchild of Markhum "Mark" L. Stansbury Sr., a Teen Town Singer himself — was an important news organ for the burgeoning choral group. It was a good marketing tool, Stansbury said, to promote the group, the goings-on, and current events.

"I remember talking to Mr. Williams," said Stansbury, whose knack for writing back in the day had become evident. "He said, 'That's a good idea.' Then he talked to David James, who was the program director [at WDIA]. He [James] said, 'I don't want it to be just for the Teen Towners. We could use this to promote WDIA events.'"

The first issue and succeeding issues were printed on an antiquated copying machine. "It was orange, because I wanted to have something different instead of white paper," said Stansbury, who was the editor for three years while he was in the Teen Town program.

On April 5, 1960, Blair T. Hunt Jr., the preeminent pastor of Mississippi Boulevard Christian Church at 974-978 Mississippi Boulevard in Memphis, Tennessee, sent a hand-written letter to WDIA at 2074 Union Avenue expressing his enjoyment of reading the Teen Town Bulletin, which was distributed widely from WDIA to school principals and guidance counselors, organizations, individuals, government officials, and others.

Blair T. Hunt Jr. wrote:

I find great enjoyment in reading the Teen Town Bulletin of radio station WDIA. I delight to learn through it the activities of a fine group of musical youngsters. Though I am in the first stage of the sacred seventies, it seems I am kept young in mind by reading of those in their tender teens through their fine bulletin.

I so hope the lads and lassies of WDIA Teen Town singers will always keep us informed of their many activities.

Thank[s] a million for the Bulletin.

Blair T. Hunt

Blair T. Hunt Jr., the son of former slaves, was born in 1888. He was a veteran of World War I, an educator, civic trailblazer, religious leader, the first pastor of Mississippi Boulevard Christian Church (1922-1973), a founding member of the Memphis Urban League, and the principal of Booker T. Washington High School in Memphis from 1932 until he retired in 1959. He died in 1978 at the age of 90. He's buried in Historic Elmwood Cemetery in

Memphis.

• • • • •

Dr. Joseph Wilson Westbrook III, a retired educator of Memphis City Schools, also penned a letter and sent it to WDIA on behalf of the Teen Town Bulletin, which he'd addressed to Markhum Stansbury. He expressed his appreciation for the choral group and their good works.

Dear Markhum:

The Teen-Town Bulletin should be an inspiration to all young people in your age group. During these times of unrest and turmoil, reading of the accomplishments of some of our young people is soothing to the soul.

The bulletin certainly gives an account of the Teen Towners activities and lets us all know what a wonderful piece of work all of you are doing. It is well written, contains selective materials and remains on a high moral and ethical plan.

Congratulations to all of the Teen-Towners. Keep up the good works and above all, thanks for including me on your mailing list.

Respectfully,
Joseph W. Westbrook, III

Dr. Westbrook died November 13, 2006, at the age of 87. He was eulogized at Mississippi Boulevard Christian

Church and interred at Historic Elmwood Cemetery in Memphis. He'd made an impact on the lives of countless students.

• • • • •

On April 4, 1960, Markhum Stansbury received a letter from Callie Lentz Stevens that she had written to him on stationary from Memphis City Schools Board of Education. Stevens mentioned that she had received the Teen Town Bulletin and had hoped to remain on the list. She also made a few suggestions.

She wrote:

Dear Mr. Stansbury:

Thank you very much for keeping me on the mailing list to receive the Teen-Town Bulletin for the past three years. I have enjoyed reading the news of Teen-Town and I hope my name will remain on the list.

The Bulletin is an excellent one for the teen-age reader. Since I work with teen-agers daily, I am very much interested in what goes on in the teen-age world. In teen-age vernacular, one might say that I am just nosy. Please consider this nosiness as concern for the Youth of our city.

My only constructive criticism of the Bulletin is on its format. I would suggest that more time be given toward making the Bulletin attractive as well as informative. There has not been enough improvement

Wiley Henry

in this area in the three years of publication.
Congratulations on your third anniversary!

Sincerely yours,
Mrs. C. Lentz Stevens

Callie Lentz Stevens was born November 4, 1926, and died July 9, 2022. She was 95 years old. A Rosary and Mass of the Resurrection were held Saturday, July 23, at Cathedral of Immaculate Inception, 1695 Central Avenue in Memphis. She is buried at Calvary Cemetery at 1663 Elvis Presley Boulevard, also in Memphis.

29

Awards, Honors, Citations

Andrew Charles "A.C." Williams Jr.'s work ethic was widely known. He'd juggled a career in radio, taught school, mentored students, launched a choral group, created opportunities for them to express their creativity, served his community and the church, and left an enduring legacy that speaks to his humanity, his benevolence, and his service to God's people — even the least of them.

The impact that he'd made in the community and beyond, and throughout his life, warranted special recognition — not that he sought it for selfish reasons, but because he earned it for being unselfish. Throughout his career, he was honored, cited for his achievements, and tapped to receive awards, certificates, and proclamations by various representatives in government, business, church, and organizations.

His compassion for the people in his community was heartfelt and reciprocated by others. Judge Carolyn Wade Blackett of Criminal Court Division IV said it best in 1995 when she wrote Williams a note: "Thank you for your support and encouragement. You will always be a very 'special' person to me. And I thank God for allowing us to have the pleasure of knowing each other. Keep me in your prayers as I will you."

United States House of Representatives

PROCLAMATION

By

Congressman Harold Ford

WHEREAS, Mr. A. C. "Moohah" Williams is deserving of recognition for his many achievements and numerous contributions within the community, and

WHEREAS, Mr. A. C. "Moohah" Williams has displayed unrelenting dedication in the field of Communications and has served as WDIA Radio Station's "morning wake-up man" for 29 years, and

WHEREAS, Mr. A. C. "Moohah" Williams is the pioneer of black radio broadcasting in Memphis and has been a fixture at the nation's oldest black-oriented radio station for many years, and

WHEREAS, Mr. A. C. "Moohah" Williams has performed his duty as Community Affairs Director at WDIA with utmost efficiency, diligence and professionalism, and

WHEREAS, Mr. A. C. "Moohah" Williams is a community activist with a strong desire to assure that the Youth of our community have a fair and equitable chance of fulfilling their goals, and

WHEREAS, Mr. A. C. "Moohah" Williams, through his outstanding leadership ability, organized the Teen Town Singers. This effort has provided college scholarships to kids for the attainment of their academic achievements, and

WHEREAS, Mr. A. C. "Moohah" Williams is an active member of Salem-Gilfield Baptist Church where he is a Deacon, Chairman of the Trustee Board, Sunday School Teacher and Director of the Wednesday night prayer meetings, and

WHEREAS, Mr. A. C. "Moohah" Williams, through his hard work and obvious potential, is the recipient of many awards and honors.

NOW BE IT THEREFORE RESOLVED, that I, HAROLD FORD, Member of Congress, join with you as you are honored on this 1st day of August, 1981 having set my hand and caused the great seal of the Congress of the United States to become affixed in Memphis, Tennessee.

HAROLD FORD
Member of Congress

The State of Tennessee
By the Honorable
NED R. McWHERTER
Speaker of the House of Representatives

Greetings: Be it hereby known that

ANDREW C. WILLIAMS

in recognition of outstanding service to the state, and extraordinary interest in Governmental processes has been appointed

An Honorary Member

Tennessee House of Representatives

and is hereby entitled to all of the honors and privileges of the
office, and to the display of this certificate

Given under my hand, this

30TH day of JULY, 1981

NED R. McWHERTER
SPEAKER OF THE HOUSE
OF REPRESENTATIVES

PRESENTED BY

NED R. McWHERTER
MEMBER OF THE HOUSE
OF REPRESENTATIVES

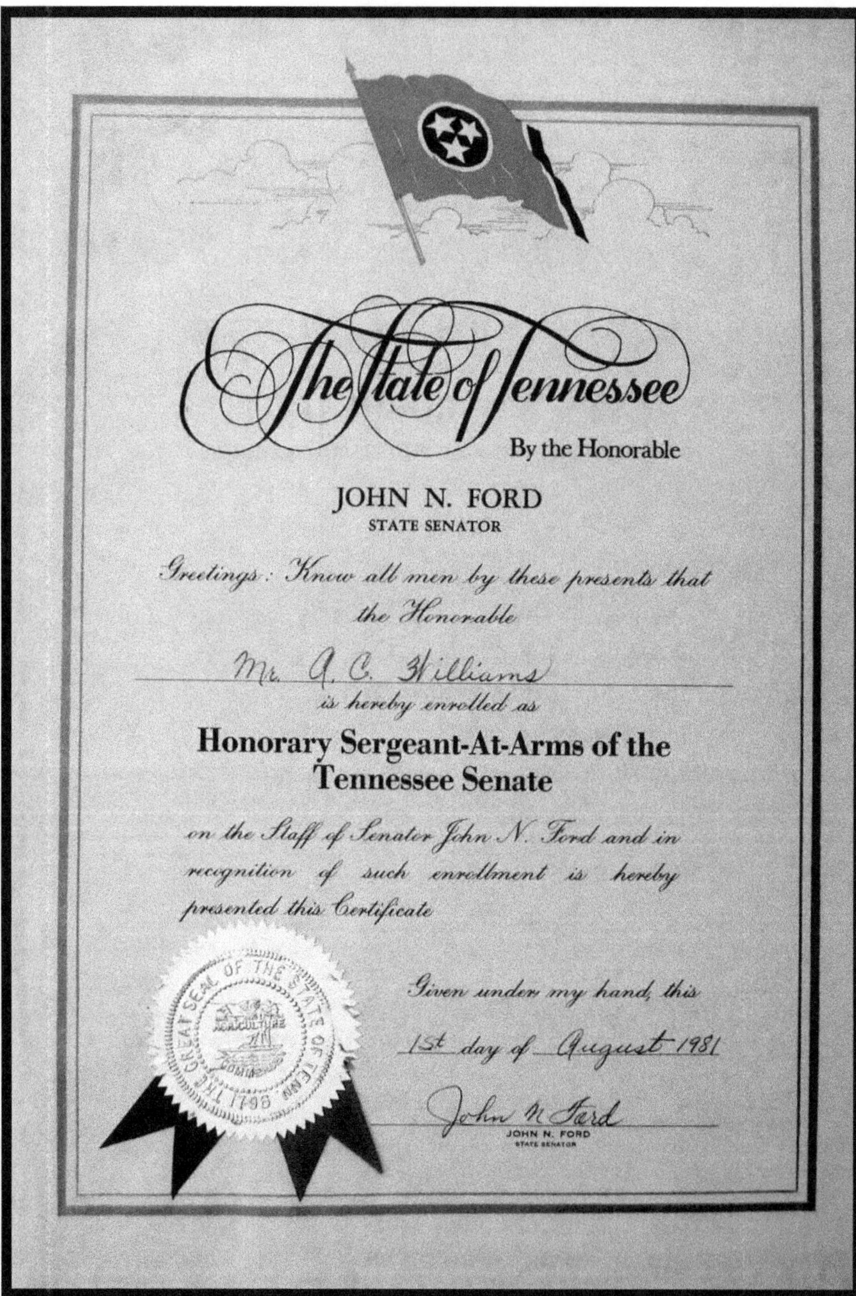

The State of Tennessee
By the Honorable
JOHN N. FORD
STATE SENATOR
Greetings: Know all men by these presents that the Honorable
Mr. A. C. Williams
is hereby enrolled as
Honorary Sergeant-At-Arms of the Tennessee Senate
on the Staff of Senator John N. Ford and in recognition of such enrollment is hereby presented this Certificate
Given under my hand, this
1st day of August 1981
John N Ford
JOHN N. FORD
STATE SENATOR

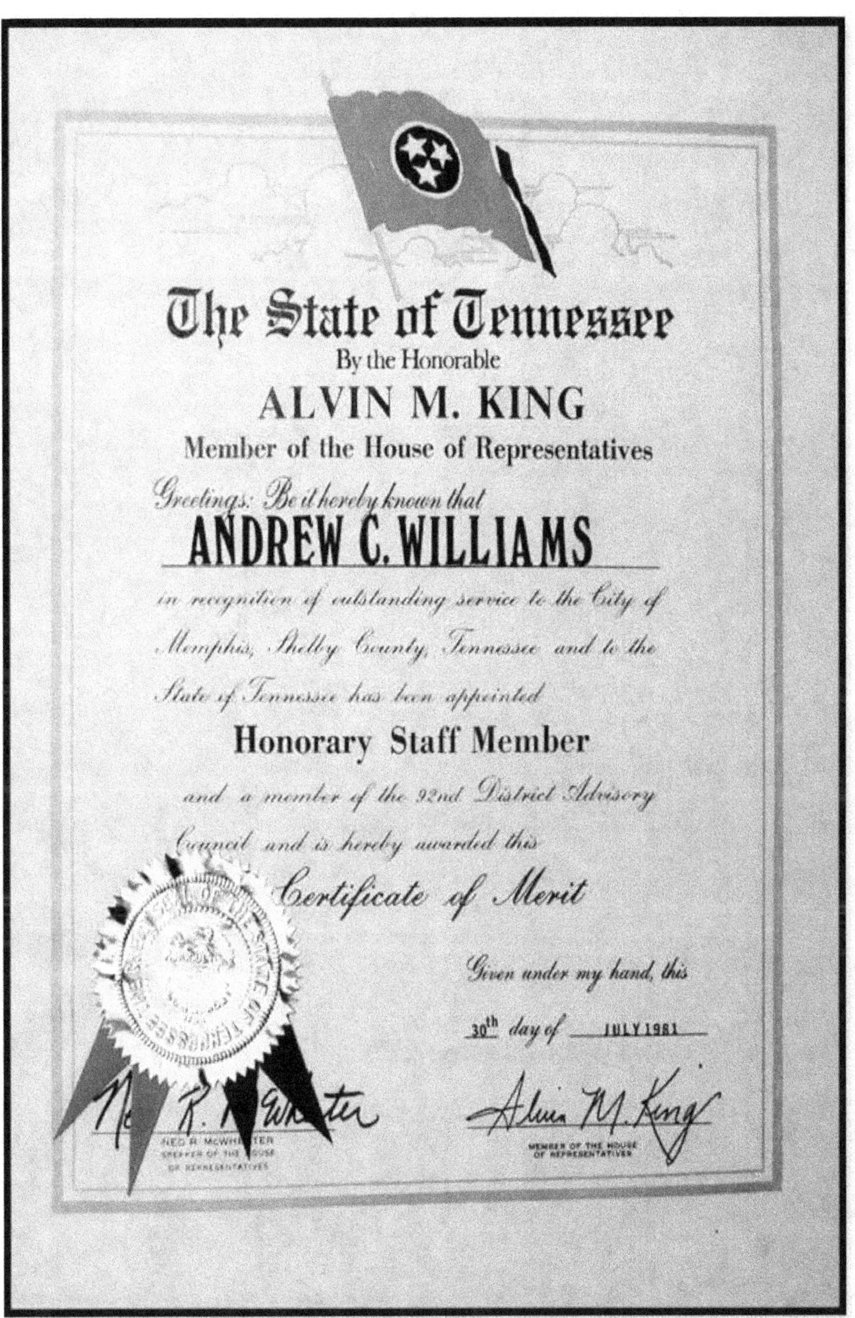
The State of Tennessee
By the Honorable
ALVIN M. KING
Member of the House of Representatives
Greetings: Be it hereby known that
ANDREW C. WILLIAMS
in recognition of outstanding service to the City of
Memphis, Shelby County, Tennessee and to the
State of Tennessee has been appointed
Honorary Staff Member
and a member of the 92nd District Advisory
Council and is hereby awarded this
Certificate of Merit
Given under my hand, this
30th day of JULY 1981
NED R. McWHIRTER
SPEAKER OF THE HOUSE
OF REPRESENTATIVES
MEMBER OF THE HOUSE
OF REPRESENTATIVES

SHELBY COUNTY GOVERNMENT

PROCLAMATION

By The Mayor

WHEREAS, Thousands of our county's radio listeners have awakened to the familiar voice of A. C. "Moohah" Williams, WDIA's most beloved disc jockey for 31 years; and

WHEREAS, For 17 years, the voice of Mr. Williams has followed Memphians to work and school and has helped them get started with their morning chores with his popular characters, Uncle Hints, Uncle Pete Prim, Benny the Bag Boy and Sin Killin' Jackson; and

WHEREAS, Although A. C. "Moohah" Williams is best known for his morning radio show, he is also recognized as a community and youth leader because of his enthusiastic work with local high school students, particularly for his radio group, the Teen Town Singers, and his lectures to high school groups; and

WHEREAS, Mr. Williams is also a deeply religious man and is an active member of the Salem-Gilfield Baptist Church where he is a Deacon, chairman of the trustee borad, teaches Sunday school and directs prayer meetings; and

WHEREAS, It is because of this sincere concern for our community's youth and adults and for the example of his belief in God and cheerful optimism that A. C. "Moohah" Williams will remain one of the most highly respected and loved characters in our county.

NOW, THEREFORE, I, William N. Morris, Jr., Mayor of Shelby County, Tennessee, do hereby proclaim Saturday, August 1, 1981, as

A. C. "MOOHAH" WILLIAMS DAY

in our county and urge all citizens to join in commending Mr. Williams for his years of service to our community and to WDIA and express our best wishes and fondness of him for the concern he has shown us all in the past.

IN WITNESS WHEREOF, I HAVE HEREUNTO SET MY HAND AND CAUSED THE SEAL OF SHELBY COUNTY TO BE AFFIXED THIS 30TH DAY OF JULY, 1981.

WILLIAM N. MORRIS, JR
Shelby County Mayor

THE STATE OF TENNESSEE

By **Lamar Alexander**, Governor, on behalf of the people of Tennessee

To the Honorable *Andrew C. Williams*

WHEREAS, reposing special trust and confidence in your patriotism, valor and fidelity, I do by these presents constitute and appoint you

COLONEL
Aide de Camp, Governor's Staff

to rank as such from the date of this commission and to hold such office under the conditions prescribed by law.

Given under my hand and the Seal of the State of Tennessee at the Capitol in Nashville, this _____ day of _______ in the year of our Lord, one thousand nine hundred and _______.

Lamar Alexander
Governor

Gentry Crowell
Secretary of State

C. H. Wallace
Adjutant General

An African American Heritage
"Living Legend Award"

Presented to

A. C. Williams

Because we remember and appreciate all that you did to make life better in the Memphis & Shelby County areas for the Sons and Daughters of Africa.

Awarded by

"The LaSimba Players" ~ New Sardis Missionary Baptist Church
on this 28th day of February, 1999

Dr. L. LaSimba M. Gray, Jr.
Senior Minister

Erma L. Clanton
Erma L. Clanton
Minister of Drama

OFFICE OF THE MAYOR

CITY OF CHICAGO

RICHARD M. DALEY
MAYOR

October 10, 1996

Dear Mr. Williams:

Thank your for the article from *The Commercial Appeal*. Your thoughtfulness is greatly appreciated.

I believe that it is important that improvements to this historic neighborhood be given due consideration as Chicago makes its plans for the 21st century.

Best wishes.

Sincerely,

Mayor

Mr. A.C. Williams
1733 Union Avenue, #505
Memphis, Tennessee 38104

State of Tennessee

House of Representatives
Proclamation

Whereas, it is important that the members of this General Assembly should honor those venerable Tennesseans whose dedication to the young people of our state serves as a model for others to emulate; and

Whereas, Mr. A.C. Williams of Memphis is one such outstanding person, who in 1949 founded the Teen-Town Singers, a group of high school and junior high school students who for 21 years had their own musical program on Radio Station WDIA; and

Whereas, a biology teacher at Manassas High School at the time, Mr. Williams later teamed with the late Cathryn Rivers Johnson, who served as co-director and pianist of the group; and

Whereas, Teen-Town singers were encouraged to pursue a college education after completing high school, and were awarded scholarships; today, over 200 former Tenn-Town Singers reside in and contribute to the betterment of the Memphis community, a trait they learned as a direct result of Mr. Williams' influence; and

Whereas, those City leaders who have been tutored under the skillful hand of A.C. Williams include: Fred Davis, a member of the first city council, first minority council chairman and an insurance executive; Mark L. Stansbury, an executive assistant to the president of the University of Memphis and himself the former interim president of Shelby State Community College; Barbara Swearengen-Holt, a member of the Memphis City Council; Dan Ward, a member of the Memphis International Airport Board of Directors; James Swearengen, a Circuit Court Judge; and Rufus Jones, a former member of the Tennessee House of Representatives, owner of Jones Big Star Supermarket, and REJ & Associates, Management Consultants/Government Relations; and

Whereas, others influenced by Mr. Williams are: Dr. Mose Yvonne Hooks, Vice President of Shelby State Community College; Dr. Ada Shotwell, Vice President and Dean of State Technical Institute at Memphis; Dr. Joyce Weddington, a specialist with the Memphis City Board of Education; Dr. Marie Milam, Director of Computer Projects with the Memphis Urban League; and Dr. Freda Williams, also a specialist with the Memphis City Board of Education; and

Whereas, it is not often that a man of A.C. Williams' stature walks among us, and it is most fitting that he be so deservedly honored; now, therefore,

I, Jimmy Naifeh, Speaker of the House of Representatives of the One-Hundredth General Assembly of the State of Tennessee, at the request of and in conjunction with Representative Barbara Cooper, do hereby proclaim that we honor Mr. A.C. Williams for his prodigious contributions to the people of Memphis and extend to him our best wishes for every future success.

Proclaimed in Nashville, Tennessee on this the 21st day of August, 1997.

SPEAKER OF THE HOUSE OF REPRESENTATIVES

REPRESENTATIVE BARBARA COOPER
86TH HOUSE DISTRICT

State of Tennessee

House of Representatives
Proclamation

Whereas, it is fitting that this General Assembly recognize those talented individuals who have brought great acclaim and honor to the State of Tennessee; and

Whereas, on August 31, 2002, the alumni of the Teen Town Singers will gather for a Labor Day weekend reunion coordinated by a steering committee composed of former members of the WDIA Teen Towners; activities include a brunch and a dinner on Saturday at the Wilson World; participants will attend church services on Sunday at Salem-Gilfield MBC; and

Whereas, founded while A. C. Williams, retired WDIA radio personality, was teaching at Manassas High School, the Teen Town Singers started with about thirty students from Manassas and eventually grew to include approximately fifteen schools in Memphis and Shelby County; and

Whereas, Mr. Williams and the late Mrs. Cathryn Rivers Johnson, who served as co-director/pianist for about fifteen years, advanced the group from an unknown chorus to a position of high acclaim throughout the WDIA eight-state listening area; William Thaw Jones served as the group's first pianist, and Evelyn Ayers was the pianist when the group was disbanded in 1970; and

Whereas, from 1949 to 1970, Saturday morning listeners of AM1070/WDIA could tune in to the voice of high school students singing contemporary tunes; and

Whereas, more than $75,000 in scholarships were granted to Teen Towners who would not have been able to attend college otherwise; many of these teens became today's ministers, teachers, principals, politicians, recording stars, attorneys, executives, and other model citizens; and

Whereas, there are more than seven hundred Teen Town alumni; among them are former City Council Chairman and Insurance Executive Fred Davis, who is Co-Chairman along with retired educator Allene Coleman McGuire; and

Whereas, other Teen Towners include former State Representative Rufus Jones, Bishop John R. Buntyn, Glenda Greer Mitchell, Dr. Ada Lee Shotwell, singer Carla Thomas, Assistant to the President, The University of Memphis, Mark Stansbury, attorney Samuel Perkins, Judge James Swearengen, City Councilwoman Barbara Swearengen-Holt, and retiree M. J. Cooper, secretary for the reunion; and

Whereas, highly deserving of recognition are those original members of the Teen Town Singers: Allene Coleman McGuire, Gloria Tuggle, Norma Griffin, Jesse Neely, Fannie Coleman, and James Swearengen; and

Whereas, each former member of the Teen Town Singers is wholly committed to the noble precepts that have earned Tennessee recognition as the "Volunteer State" and should be specially recognized; now, therefore,

I, Jimmy Naifeh, Speaker of the House of Representatives of the One Hundred Second General Assembly of the State of Tennessee, at the request of and in conjunction with Representative Lois DeBerry, do hereby proclaim that we honor and commend the alumni of the Teen Town Singers and wish them much success and happiness in the years to come.

Proclaimed in Nashville, Tennessee on this the 28th day of August, 2002.

OFFICE OF THE MAYOR

CITY OF CHICAGO

RICHARD M. DALEY
MAYOR

October 10, 1996

Dear Mr. Williams:

Thank you for the article from *The Commercial Appeal.* Your thoughtfulness is greatly appreciated.

I believe that it is important that improvements to this historic neighborhood be given due consideration as Chicago makes its plans for the 21st century.

Best wishes.

Sincerely,

Mayor

Mr. A.C. Williams
1733 Union Avenue, #505
Memphis, Tennessee 38104

BILL FRIST
TENNESSEE

COMMITTEES

Banking, Housing and Urban Affairs
Budget
Labor and Human Resources
Small Business

United States Senate

WASHINGTON, DC 20510-4205

September 26, 1995

Mr. A. C. Williams
1733 Union Avenue, Apartment 505
Memphis, Tennessee 38104-6134

Dear Mr. Williams:

Thank you for contacting me regarding your opposition to
S. 1137, the "Fairness in Musical Licensing Act of 1995." I am
sorry about the delay in responding and appreciate your patience
with regard to the timeliness of my response. I am honored to
serve you in the Senate, and it is a privilege to respond to your
concerns.

This legislation was introduced in the Senate on August 9,
1995 by Senator Craig Thomas, and has been referred to the Senate
Judiciary Committee for consideration. The House Judiciary
Committee is currently considering H.R. 789, which is a companion
bill identical to S. 1137.

As you know, Tennessee is home to some of the most talented
songwriters in the country, and some of the provisions of this
legislation would directly affect those who, through their hard
work, are collecting royalties from their music copyrights.
Should S. 1137 come before the Senate, I will keep your concerns
in mind, and will work to protect the intellectual property
rights of songwriters.

Again, thank you for taking the time to express your
concerns. As I serve you in the Senate, I hope that you will

MAYOR'S OFFICE
EARL S. LUCAS, MAYOR

ALDERMAN
LAWRENCE THOMPSON
MRS. ANNYCE CAMPBELL
HAROLD WARD
HERMON JOHNSON
FELIX TATE

P.O. BOX DRAWER "H"
MOUND BAYOU, MISS.
38762
PHONE (601) 741-2191

MISS MINNIE L. FISHER
CLERK & TAX COLLECTOR

ALFRED THOMPSON
CHIEF OF POLICE

GREETINGS

We should like to take this opportunity to extend a hearty welcome to all sponsors, participants and guests of the ninth (9th) Annual Delta Talent Search.

You have our full support in your efforts to perpetuate an enrichment program for our youth. Such expressions of talents bring out the natural endowments of our youth and thus exhibit the artistic aptitudes which will give them a favorable opportunity to contribute to the growth of our prosperity.

It is our sincere hope that you will continue in your efforts to give our youth the inspiration needed to pave the way for the accomplishment of their goals and objectives.

You have our very best wishes for a pleasant and profitable day.

Earl S. Lucas, Mayor
Minnie L. Fisher, City Clerk
Annyce Campbell, Alderwoman
Hermon Johnson, Alderman
Lawrence Thompson, Alderman
Harold Ward, Alderman
Felix Tate, Alderman

HERITAGE TOURS, INC.
280 Hernando Street
Memphis, TN 38126
(901)527-3427   FAX (901)527-8784

October 18, 2004

Mr. A. C. Williams
1733 Union Ave #505
Memphis, TN 38104

Dear Mr. Williams,

Congratulations! You have been selected to receive the W.C. Handy Heritage Awards on the occasion of the 131st Birthday Anniversary of W.C. Handy, "Father of the Blues," sponsored by the W.C. Handy Museum and Heritage Tours. The awards will be held on Sunday, November 21, 2004 at 6:00 p.m. at Isaac Hayes Music*Food*Passion.

You will receive the special "Memphis Music Legacy Award" for the vital role that it plays in the Memphis community in preserving this city's rich musical heritage. Joining us at the awards will be members of the W.C. Handy family from New York.

Please confirm your attendance by contacting our office at Heritage Tours (527-3427). Also, please send a photograph and biographical information to be included in the Souvenir Booklet.

Sincerely,

Elaine Turner
W.C. Handy Birthday Committee

ET/hb

THE CRIMINAL COURT OF TENNESSEE
THIRTIETH JUDICIAL DISTRICT AT MEMPHIS
201 POPLAR
MEMPHIS, TENNESSEE 38103

CAROLYN WADE BLACKETT
JUDGE OF DIVISION IV

February 22, 1995

Mr. A. C. Williams
1733 Union Avenue, Suite 505
Memphis, TN 38104

Dear A. C.:

Congratulations on a job well done. Very few of us will be fortunate enough to make great contributions to this community as you have over the years.

Sincerely,

Judge Carolyn Wade Blackett

CWB/bea

Enclosure

JAMES E. SWEARENGEN
JUDGE

FOURTH DIVISION
THIRTIETH JUDICIAL CIRCUIT
STATE OF TENNESSEE

SHELBY COUNTY COURTHOUSE
140 ADAMS AVENUE
MEMPHIS, TENNESSEE 38103

May 25, 1990

Mr. A. C. Williams
1733 Union Avenue, #505
Memphis, Tennessee 38104

Dear Mr. Williams:

Please find enclosed my check in the amount of $35.00. I am also enclosing a copy of your announcement which I have taken the liberty to modify by adding some language at the bottom of the page.

Let me know if I can be of any assistance to you in this effort.

I have talked to a number of the "clan" and they are all excited about the idea.

Affectionately yours,

"*Swearengen*"

James E. Swearengen

JES/jp

Enclosure

Shelby County Board Of Commissioners
Be it hereby known that the Honorable
A.C. "Moohah" Williams
In recognition of outstanding
service to Shelby County and extraordinary
interest in the Governmental process
has been appointed
Honorary Shelby County Commissioner
and is hereby entitled to all of the honors
and privileges of the office, and to the display
of the certificate.
Given under my hand,
this 1st day of August 1981
COMMISSIONER
CHARLES R. PERKINS
Chairman

30

The Complete Roster
THE TEEN TOWN SINGERS

A
Rev. Harold Adams
Claranice Smith Al-Ghani
Paulette Anthony
Rosemary McKissick
Archibald
Magnolia Armstrong
Evelyn-Geeter Ayers

B
Elsie Lewis Bailey
Barbara Beans
Sandra A. Bell
Regina Bennett
Shelby Brooks Bennett
Delores Downey Blair
Ann Kirk Blakman
Willie J. Blevins Blue
Mary Campbell Bohannon
Ruth Britt Booker
Archie Aldophus Branch
Laneatha Collins Branch
Bernice Smith Brandon
Juanita Bridges Brassel
Dianne Rice Brewster
Diane Brewster
J.B. Brooks

Annie Thurman Broom
Dorsey Broome
Brenda McKinney Brothers
Fred L. Brown
Lois Joyner Brown
Ruth Oliver Bryant
Olubayo Bunchinji
(Johnnie Ruth Taylor)
Rev. John Ray Buntyn, Jr.
Rudy Buntyn

C
Amanda Battles Campbell
Marilyn Campbell
Charles Cannon
George S. Carr
Benjamin Carroll
Wilhelmina Carter
Glenda Collins Catron
Deborah McCullum Childs
Clarence Christian
Joe Ann Branch Clark
Pinkie Hunt Clark
Brenda Carwill Clark-Cowlie
Mary Bridges Clay
Diane Coburn
Barbara Hill Cole

Bernice Rosebud Cole
Clementine Cole
Beverly Coleman
Fannie Coleman
Barbara Gatlin Collins
Lillian Fields Cooper
Mary J. Cooper
Melissa Cooper
Cheryl Fanion Cotton
Isaac Craigen III
Clyde E. Crawford
Imogene Tina Bryant
Crawford
John Crawford
James Crittenden
William H. Cross
Barbara J. Smith Cummings
Patricia Cummins
Marie Rice Cunningham

D

Delores Burton Davis
Fred Davis
Rosie Christian Dennis
Annie M. Dodson
Anita Dorsey
Rev. Semiller Douglas
Clifton Drake

E

James Easley
Lester-Mitchell Echols
Levata Edwards
Yvette K. Lewis Eleby
Edith Bobo Eley
Judith Nelson Epps
Beverly Anne Eubanks

F

Fannie Farmer
Marzie Fayne
Jewel Fifer
Dr. William H. Fleming
Jassie Ford
Lois Burnley Forson
Nova Montgomery Fulton

G

Robert Garner
Glenneth Gilmore
Pearl Ingram Gipson
Georgia Bland Gleese
Marjean Goodman
Willie Green
Al Greene
Bonnie Greene
Norma Jean Griffin
Sandra Griffin

H

Jacqueline Hall
Josephine Hall
Robert Hall
Allen Hamilton Jr.
Sandra J. Hamilton
Norma Hampton
Diane Warren Hardaway
Dr. Fred O. Hardy
Wilma Hayden
Isaac Hayes
Stephen Hayes
Dorothy Herenton
Evelyn Hester
Barbara Hightower
Donald Hines

Teen Town Singers

Irene Hines
Pearl Westbrooks Hines
Gloria Hitchings
Myra Farmer Holland
Barbara Swearengen Holt
Sandra Wilson Hosey
Brenda House
Josephine Houston
Thelma Perry Howell
Barbara Howze
Dorothy J. Hudson
Lillie Hughey

J

Blancha Harris Jackson
Carolyn J. Jackson
Claudia Ivy Jackson
Lillie Moore Jackson
Bennie Jenkins
Catherine Rivers Johnson
Glenn L. Johnson
Mary Campbell Johnson
Beverly Jean Bankston Jones
Deborah Moten Jones
Mary Lee Jones
Mildred Harrington Jones
Rufus Jones
Willie Jones

K

Frances Burnett Kelley

L

Genthia Collins Lacy
Jean Lavender
Geraldine Riley Lee
George Lesseur

Diane Horner Little
Anita Louis

M

Samantha L. Macklin
Herbert Marshall
Marilyn Martin
Elanor Neely Mason
Rev. Robert Matthews
Eugene McClaren
Buddie Taylor McGlaun
Allene Coleman McGuire
Timothy McGuire
Queen Money McKinney
Aretha Townsel McNeal
Linda Harrell McNeil
Shirley Duckett McRee
Patricia Jackson McWright
Rev. Harold Middlebrook
Marie Austin Milam
Carolyn Milan
Marla Milan
Patricia W. Milan
Davis Mimes
Elizabeth E. Mincy
Carol Willis Mitchell
Clarence Mitchell
Geraldine Seay Mitchell
Glenda Grear Mitchell
Joyce Mitchell
Juanita Blake Mitchum
Caroline Montgomery
Patricia Echols Montgomery
Anita Walton Moore
Bonnie Riley Moore
Charlie Moore
Rev. Freedie Moore

Paola Green Moore
Rholedia McGuire Morgan
Alfred Motlow
Eddie Murphy

N

Joyce Winston Nash
Alma Neal
Jesse Neeley
Clarise Nelson
Gwen Nelson
James Nelson
Judith Nelson
Gloria Nightingale
James C. Nolan
Winnoka Phifer Norfleet
Mildred Rayner Norman

O

Charles L. Oliver Jr.
Rita Kilgore Owens

P

Grant Parham Jr.
Arnetta Anderson Parrish
Col. Arthur T. Patterson
(retired)
Drucilla Ingram Patterson
Joan Williams Patterson
Proteon Taylor Paulk
Moses Peace
Samuel Peace Jr.
Samuel Perkins
Robert Phifer
Joy Plunkett
Sylvia Buntyn Poindexter
Estella Middlebrook Powell

Q

Gwendolyn Townsel Quirley

R

Apostle John L. Ragland
Jessie Merriwether Randle
Wanda D. McKay Randle
Dalestine Shelby Rayford
Betty Dancy Reed
Bettie Nickens Richardson
Bonnie Richardson
Ann Brown Robertson
Josephine Williams Robertson
Marian Robinson
Phyllis Robinson
Raymond Robinson
Samuel Robinson
Eddie Rodman
Thelma Lemmons Rogers
Elzie Rosebud
Patricia Ryans

S

Katherine Sanders
Lurene Johnson Sanders
Rodell Sanders
Amanda Bridges Sargent
Thelma Shannon
Ada C. Lee Shotwell
Betty Patterson Sims
Shirley Sims
Betty Smith
Deborah L. Smith
Emma Blue Smith
Gloria J. Smith
Jerry Smith
Tyrone Smith

Markhum L. Stansbury
Almella Starks
Jackie Staten
Lovell Stringfellow
Freddie Strong
Anita Suggs
Williams Sumlin
James Swearingen
Irma J. Dailey Sydes

T
Thomas Tabor
Jennie Thurmon Tate
Carolyn M. Ghomas Taylor
Earlice Taylor
Harry L. Taylor
Beverly Buntyn Thomas
Carla Thomas
Cheryl Thomas
Donald Thomas
Harold Thomas
Jean Thomas
Joyce Thomas
Lillie A. Thomas
Marvell Thomas
Pearline Crawford Thomas
Phyllis Taylor Thomas
Robert Thomas
Rene Thomas-Lessard
Evelyn Cole Thorpe
Betty J. Todd
Diane Towsend
Mary Alyce Patterson Tubbs
Melva Houston Tucker
Gloria Tuggle
Doris C. Tunstall

U
Willie J. Underwood
Freddie Ushrea

W
Joyce Brown Waddington
Daniel Ward
Gloria Massey Ward
Samella Ward
Mildred Cash Warner
Elizabeth Washington
Linda Tatum Weathers
Alvin White
Marian Hassell Whitson
Percy Wiggins
Spencer Wiggins
Andrew C. Williams
Carol Owens Williams
Diane Dancy Williams
Freda Williams
Jackie Williams
Jacquelyn McKinney Williams
Mildred Scott Williams
Shasta Williams
Vernita Williams
Dianne Williams
Charlezetta Whitehead
Williamson
Garland Willingham
Dardean Woods Willis
Dorothy J. Wilson
Barbara Griffin Winfield
Emmett J. Winters
Clarence Withers
Willie M. Woods
Ilien Wooten
Barbara Perry Wright

31

The Teen Town Singers' Song List

"DOWN IN OLE MEMPHIS TOWN"
(Theme Song)

In Spring it's Cotton time
And o what joy sublime
The King and Queen they crown
Down in ole Memphis town

In fall the Tri-State fair,
Three states will sure be there
Miss., Ark., and Tenn. Are found
Down in ole Memphis town

Summertime is swim time
Everything is so fine
But all the fine dames
Love an old ball game

In Winter folks stay in
Till nine or half past ten
That's where I'm always found
Down in ole Memphis time

Repeat: DOWN IN OLE MEMPHIS TOWN

THE "SPIRITUALS

"EZEKIEL SAW DE WHEEL"

Chorus:

Ezekiel saw de' wheel, Way up in de middle of de air,
Ezekiel saw de' wheel, Way in de middle of de air,
De big wheel run by faith, and de lil wheel run by de grace
of God, A wheel in a wheel, Way in de middle of the air.

Better mine my sister how you walk on de cross,
Way in de middle of de air,

Yo foot might slip, an yo' soul be los',
Way in de middle of de air.

Repeat Chorus

"KING JESUS IS A LISTENIN'"

Chorus:

King Jesus is a listenin' all night long,
King Jesus is a listenin' all night long,
King Jesus is a listenin' all night long,
To hear some sinner pray.

That gospel train is comin', A rumblin' thru the lan',
I hear them wheels a-hummin', Get ready to board that train;

I know I been converted, I'll tell you the reason why,
I'm afraid my Lord might call me, and I wouldn't be ready to die.

Repeat Chorus:

"ALL NIGHT, ALL DAY"

Chorus

All night, all day, Angels watching over me my Lord
All night, all day, Angels watching over me.

Repeat

LEAD: One of these mornings it won't be long
(Angels watching over me my Lord)

LEAD: You're gonna look for me and I'll be gone
(Angels watching over me)

Repeat Chorus

LEAD: One of these mornings bright and fair
(Angels watching over me my Lord)

LEAD: I'm gonna take my wings and cleave the air
(Angels watching over me)

Repeat Chorus

"GOOD NEWS, THE CHARIOT'S COMING"

Chorus:

(LADIES) Good news, (GUYS) Good news, (ALL) Chariot's
coming
(LADIES) Good news, (GUYS) Good news, (ALL) Chariot's
coming
(LADIES) Good news, (GUYS) Good news, (ALL) Chariot's
coming
(ALL) And I don't want you to leave-a me behind!

Repeat

(LADIES) There's a long white robe in the Heavens I know
(HOLD)
(GUYS) There's a long white robe in the Heavens I know
(GUYS) There's a long white robe in the Heavens I know
(GUYS) There's a long white robe in the Heavens I know
(ALL) And I don't want you to leave-a me behind!

Chorus Twice

(LADIES) There's a starry crown in the Heavens I know (HOLD)
(GUYS) There's a starry crown in the Heavens I know
(GUYS) There's a starry crown in the Heavens I know
(GUYS) There's a starry crown in the Heavens I know
(ALL) And I don't want you to leave-a me behind!

Chorus Twice

(ENDING) And I don't want you to leave-a me behind! (CUT
OFF)

"BLUE HEAVEN"

When whip-po-wills call,
And evening is nigh,
I hurry to my blue heaven.

You turn to the right
A little white light
Will lead you to my blue heaven.

You'll see a smiling face
A fireplace, a cozy room,
A little nest that nestles
Where the roses bloom.

Just Molly and me
And baby makes three
We're happy in my blue heaven

When whip-po-wills call, (Whip-po-wills)
And evening is nigh (Die-de-die-de-i)
I hurry to my blue heaven.

You turn to the right
A little white light
Will lead you to my Blue Heaven

You'll see a smiling face,
A fireplace (hand claps twice)
(Ooh) – Cozy rooms
A little nest that nestles
Where (Oh a nest that nestles)
Where the roses bloom.

Molly and me,
Baby makes three,
(The stuff is here and it's mellow in my-mellow in my Blue
Heaven)
(da de de ah do dah)
Molly and me,
(We're happy, just we three)

"HONEY DRIPPER"

Boy-o-wheel the honey dripper,
He's a killer, the honey dripper,
Soft, Sweet, Hot, He's a solid ole cat,
Really, a mellow help-cat.
He jumps and swings
He riffs and rides.
He's the king of swing,
He's the height of Jive,
You did that cat and jump for joy.

You did that lick, You dig that beat,
You get knocked out right off your feet.
One, two, three, four, five, six
That cat can jam, or riff, or swing that hot licks,
Boy, He sure does jump for joy.

Lit-did-de, He's a killer
Lit-did-de, The honey driller
(loud) Hoy, Hoy, Hoy, (soft) hoy, hoy, hoy, hoy
Lit-did-de, He's a ripper
Lit-did-de, The honey dripper
(loud) Hoy, Hoy, Hoy, (soft) hoy, hoy, hoy, hoy
For darling, I am growing older,
Darling, I am growing older.

Dot di did-dle li-dot,
Dot di did-dle li-dot,

Repeat
You dig that cat, and jump for joy,
The Honey Dripper!

"COTTON"

Cotton, my heart's all wrapped up in Cotton,
Its snow white charm takes me back where I belong,
Along the Mississippi shores.

I hear the bottoms call-ing Cotton,
The South is rich in its Cotton,
No false alarm, It's a mighty pretty song,
The southern cotton maidens know.

Bridge:

I guess the Lord was partial to the southland;
To give it the cotton and the corn;
The bright sunshine, It's yours and mine,
And that's where I was born.

In the land of Cotton,

I sing a love song of Cotton,
And that is why that no matter how I try;
I can't forget the South's my home.

The Cotton South's My Home!

32. CONSTITUTION

Name: The name of the organization shall be The Teen Town Singers.

Purpose: The purpose of the organization is as follows:
1. To retain the heritage of The Teen Town Singers as established and perpetuated by its founder and subsequent members;
2. To give young people an outlet for creative expression;
3. To perform community service projects;
4. To create a link between the organization and its members by drawing on the talent and resources of members who are located throughout the country.

Meetings: The Teen Town Singers will meet on a ________ basis.

Officers: Officers of the organization will be President, Vice President, Secretary, and Treasurer.

Membership: Membership in this organization is open to any person who was ever a member of the WDIA Teen Town Singers.

BYLAWS

ARTICLE I — NAME AND LOCATION

The name of this organization shall be The Teen Town
                Singers. It shall
have its main office in Memphis, Tennessee.
ARTICLE II — PURPOSE

The purpose of this organization is as follows:

A. To retain the heritage of The Teen Town Singers
   as established and perpetuated by its founder and
   subsequent members;
B. To give young people an outlet for creative
   expression;
C. To perform community service projects;
D. To create a link between the organization and its
   members by drawing on the talent and resources
   of members who are located through the country.

ARTICLE III — MEMBERSHIP

Section 1. Eligibility

A. Membership in this organization is open to any
   person who was ever a member of the WDIA Teen
   Town Singers.
B. A condition of membership shall be the payment
   of the annual dues assessed by the organization.

Section 2. Classification

Any member who has paid annual dues for the current fiscal year will be classified as an active member.

ARTICLE IV — DUES

Annual dues shall be in the amount determined by the officers.

ARTICLE V — OFFICERS, NOMINATION AND ELECTION, TERM, AND DUTIES

Section 1. Officers

The officers of this organization shall be the president, vice president, secretary, and treasurer. Other officers may be added as required by the organization.

Section 2. Nomination and Election

The procedure for nomination and election of officers shall be as follows:

A. The nominating committee shall consist of three members appointed by the president.
B. The nominating committee shall nominate one or more candidates for each office after first obtaining permission from the nominees.
C. The nominating committee shall report to the membership prior to the election.
D. The vote shall be by ballot.
E. The election shall occur at the end of the calendar year.

F. If any office becomes vacant during the calendar year, it shall be the responsibility of the president to appoint a successor to such office to serve the remainder of the calendar year.

Section 3. Term of Office

The term of office shall be for two years and shall begin in January of each year.

Section 4. Duties of Officers

The duties of the officers of this organization shall be as follows:

A.   It shall be the duty of the president to:
1.   Preside at all regular and called meetings.
2.   Appoint all committees.
3.   Approve all expenditures, subject to the approval of the Executive Committee.
4.   Perform such other duties as pertain to the office.

B.   It shall be the duty of the vice president to:
1.   Preside at all meetings at the absence of the president and assume the duties and powers of the president in the officers' absence.
2.   Assume the presidency for the unexpired term of the president upon the resignation or removal of that officer.
3.   Plan activities and program initiatives in concert with the president.
4.   Perform such other duties as pertain to the office.

C. It shall be the duty of the secretary to:
1.   Record the minutes of all official organization meetings.
2.   Prepare the agenda for the meeting when requested by the president.
3.   Conduct the general correspondence of the organization under the general direction of the president.
4.   Maintain an accurate membership roll and take roll at all official organization meetings.

D. It shall be the duty of the treasurer to:
1.   Collect and deposit all monies belonging to the organization in conformity to the regulations established by the Executive Committee.
2.   Pay the bills in conformity with the regulations established by the Executive Committee.
3.   Present a financial report periodically to the organization and at the end of the year.
4.   Perform such duties as pertain to the office.

ARTICLE VI – COMMITTEES

Section 1. Standing Committees.

Standing committees shall be composed of a chairperson and two or more members. Appointments shall be effective at the beginning of the calendar year for a term of one year.

TEEN TOWN
WDIA
SINGERS

INDEX

INDEX

INDEX

SOURCES

The story of A.C. Williams Jr. and The Teen Town Singers was derived from several media sources and testimonies from some of the surviving Teen Town Singers themselves, including articles and news stories from the following newspapers, websites, books, etc.:

The Commercial Appeal
The Memphis Press Scimitar
Courier Magazine
The Pittsburgh Courier
The Tri-State Defender
The Memphis World
Memphis Citizen
The Silver Star News
Wikipedia
Louis Cantor's "Wheelin' on Beale"
The History Makers (Markhum "Mark" L. Stansbury Sr.)

The timeless adage of "a picture is worth a thousand words" is particularly true — for this book contains many of them of A.C. Williams Jr. and The Teen Town Singers in the early days after the choral group was founded, during their heyday, and throughout their adulthood. Collecting such photographs would've been very difficult if it had not been for a scrapbook that Mr. Williams compiled over the years that illustrated in words and photographs his eminence as a leader and the essence of the young and talented teenagers in his charge. His daughter, Joan E. Patterson, was gracious enough to loan me the scrapbook to complete this worthful project. The photographs, indeed, are worth thousands of words — thanks to the following photographers:

Ernest C. Withers
Hooks Brothers Photographers
Jaffe Commercial Photographers
Lewin-Miller
Tyrone P. Easley
Wiley Henry

ACKNOWLEDGMENTS

Had it not been for Andrew Charles "A.C." Williams Jr., a man called "Moohah" — The Mighty One — this book would not be possible. So, I thank Mr. Williams and The Teen Town Singers whose lives he cultivated and shaped into the finest specimen of men and women bar none. And of that number — more than 700 altogether — Markhum "Mark" L. Stansbury Sr., a dear friend, entrusted me to capture in words the uniqueness of Mr. Williams, who corralled inner-city teens from Black high schools in Memphis, Tennessee, and provided them a platform to reach for the stars. Many of them succeeded. As Mr. Stansbury would say, "Tell the Lord Thank You!"

ABOUT THE AUTHOR

Wiley Henry is an award-winning journalist and former deputy editor of *The Tri-State Defender* in Memphis, where he spent three decades as one of the newspaper's top reporters and editors. He also served as editor of *The Black Pages* of New Orleans and received several national, regional, and local journalism awards. His freelance contributions included stories or op-eds for *The Commercial Appeal, The Memphis Flyer, Grace Magazine,* and *The Tennessee Tribune,* a Black weekly newspaper in Nashville, Tennessee. For the Carter Malone Group, a local public relations firm, he served as a senior writer.

Wiley Henry is also a noted artist and photographer. His artwork has been marketed locally and nationally, and he's received commissions for greeting cards, posters, murals, and portraits of judges, pastors, attorneys, actors, educators, and mayors. His portrait of Madam C. J. Walker, for example, hung in the governor's mansion in Indianapolis, Indiana. Also, he has received several awards and citations for community service, including the "Volunteer of the Year" award in 2000; the "Memphis Living Legends" award in 2009, the "Lifetime Achievement Award" in 2017; "Man of the Year" in 2018, and several others.

9 798888 955135